Raising an Anxious Child

Practical Strategies Every Parent Must Know to Raise Happy and Confident Children Without Over-Parenting

Erika Miller

©Copyright 2021 – Erika Miller - All rights reserved

The content contained within this book may not be reproduced, duplicated, or transmitted without direct written permission from the author or the publisher.

Under no circumstances will any blame or legal responsibility be held against the publisher, or author, for any damages, reparation, or monetary loss due to the information contained within this book, either directly or indirectly.

Legal Notice

This book is copyright protected. This book is only for personal use. You cannot amend, distribute, sell, use, quote, or paraphrase any part, or the content within this book, without the consent of the author-publisher.

Disclaimer Notice

Please note the information contained within this document is for educational and entertainment purposes only. All effort has been executed to present accurate, up-to-date, and reliable, complete information. No warranties of any kind are declared or implied. Readers acknowledge that the author is not engaging in the rendering of legal, financial, medical, or professional advice.

Table of Contents

UNDERSTANDING ANXIETY 5

Chapter 1: The cycle of Anxiety - How Anxiety Works 6

Chapter 2: Why some people are more anxious than others 9

Chapter 3: The differences between general anxiety and specific phobias 13

Chapter 4: The difference in Child anxiety and OCD 22

Chapter 5: Anxiety and social media 27

Chapter 6: The link between anxiety and learning difficulties 31

Chapter 7: Anxiety Explanation for Kids 36

RECOGNIZING ANXIETY 40

Chapter 8: Signs and Symptoms of Anxiety in Children 41

Chapter 9: Identifying and Managing Fears, Worries, and Phobias 45

Chapter 10: Identifying and Managing Depression in your Child .. 51

Chapter 11: Identifying Social Anxiety 56

Chapter 12: Identifying Separation Anxiety 62

Chapter 13: Identifying Low self Esteem 66

Chapter 14: Identifying Stress 70

Chapter 15: Managing Frequent Nightmares 75

OVERCOMING ANXIETY 82

Chapter 16: Managing Your Anxiety While Raising Anxious Kids .. 83

Chapter 17: Specific communication skills for Parents 88

Chapter 18: Teaching Kids to Change Negative Thoughts to Positive Thoughts 93

Chapter 19: Practical Strategies to Coping with Social Anxiety 99

Chapter 20: Practical Strategies to Coping with Separation Anxiety 107

Chapter 21: Practical Strategies to Coping with Nervous Talking in groups 116

Chapter 22: Phrases for calming your anxious Child 119

Chapter 23: Learning managing Worries.. 127

Chapter 24: Managing shyness.. 137

Chapter 25: Overcoming perfectionism 141

Chapter 26: How To Help Children Who Have Anxiety About The Doctor & Shots.. 148

Chapter 27: How to help your child managing Stress................... 154

Chapter 28: How to help your child Make Friends....................... 158

Chapter 29: Help your child not to be afraid of school................ 169

Chapter 30: Help your Child During Panic attacks 173

RAISING WITH SELF LOVE.. 179

Chapter 31: Raise Yourself before you Raise your Child................180

Chapter 32: Overwhelmed Thinking 185

Chapter 33: Body Shaming 189

Chapter 34: Myths about raising an anxious child 191

PART 1

UNDERSTANDING ANXIETY

Chapter 1:
The cycle of Anxiety - How Anxiety Works

Have you ever realized that you might do something that you needed to do, but you were scared or very worried about it? Like maybe going skydiving or flying across the world to a country whose language you do not know, or maybe something more day-to-day like asking someone out on a date. It will mean leaving your comfort zone and doing something you would not usually do. If you don't do these things, when you do not confront your worries, anxiety continues to rise, which leads to what is known as the Anxiety Cycle or the Avoidance Cycle.

To experience fear is to think about a possible threat. It is trying to deal with a potential situation that you believe will go wrong. You do this by paying closer attention to any signs of imminent danger and looking internally to see how you will deal with the threat. When you experience the signs of anxiety, you think you cannot deal with the situation, so you get more anxious. This is the beginning of a vicious spiral into fear.

In the cycle of anxiety, a person refuses to face their fears, and as a result, those fears become a part of your life. Many anxiety therapies work by stopping this loop. They focus on overcoming fears rather than ignoring them.

Feeling anxious is the first step in the method. This phase starts when you are first faced with something that makes you feel uncomfortable or frightened. You tend to experience some unpleasant signs when you are faced with this. You experience signs of fear, such as pounding of the heart, butterflies in the stomach, sweating, or shaking. When you start to experience these symptoms, you want them to stop because they are so unpleasant.

The second stage is to find a way to stop the fear. When those signs of distress get too much and too uncomfortable, it is very tempting to find a means to get rid of them, and the best way to do it is to stop it. No matter what triggers them, Physical prevention is one way to do this, and it is to get out of that situation. For example, someone who does not want to go to work or attend school lessons may miss a class or call in sick to work, so they get the day to themselves. Stomping down your emotions is another method of prevention. This is when someone experiences that terror, but they find a way to suppress that discomfort or feeling that goes with it. A clear example of this is someone at a party who is very anxious and does not want to talk to people, so they drink the fear away.

The third phase of the loop is a short-term relief from fear. This means a person makes the decision not to confront their fear, and it works. They are relieved of their symptoms. Staying at home, lying on the sofa to watch TV, or just lazing about feels pretty good. The concern is that kind of relaxation is short-lived and has a price, sometimes small, sometimes hefty, attached to it. If you miss the job interview, someone else will get it. You will get bad grades if you skip too many classes. If you do not ask anyone on a date, you might miss the chance to meet your soulmate.

The fourth and final step in the cycle is long-term anxiety development. This means that you have stopped the issue that triggered the anxiety. The signs are gone, and the fear has diminished, but the feeling of anxiety keeps making appearances more and more in your everyday life.

Chapter 2:
Why some people are more anxious than others

Anxiety is a common problem in the community nowadays. It is one of the most common reasons more people are going to counseling.

Some people are over-achieving perfectionists with debilitating feelings of disappointment. Others are so worried about what their colleagues think about them that they are unable to work. Many have experienced harsh conditions in their young lives. However, others have healthy families, loving parents, and much money; in short, they are living the dream. The uptick in anxiety represents various social developments and cultural transitions that we have witnessed over the last few decades.

Anxiety, rather than depression, is the leading mental health problem for American youth, and doctors and analysts say that it is rapidly increasing.

Here are the top 10 reasons for this:

1. Gadgets are providing an unsanitary escape.

Constant access to interactive technology helps children and adults avoid uncomfortable feelings such as boredom, isolation, or depression by immersing themselves in gaming while driving or scrolling through and interacting on social media when sent to their rooms. Moreover, now we are seeing what happens when a generation has spent their childhood resisting pain. Their technology replaced chances to improve emotional resilience, and they did not learn the skills needed to deal with daily difficulties.

2. Pleasure is all the rage.

Happiness is so much stressed in our society that some parents believe they must keep their children happy at all times. When a kid is upset, his parents cheer him up. Kids grow up thinking that something has to be wrong if they do not feel happy around the clock. It causes much inner chaos. They do not realize that it is natural and safe to feel unhappy, upset, guilty, discouraged, and even furious.

3. Parents offer unreal praise.

Saying something like, "You are the quickest runner on the squad," or, "You are the smartest kid in your class," does not build self-esteem. Instead, it places pressure on children to live up to their given labels. This can lead to a debilitating fear of disappointment or rejection.

4. Parents are stuck in a rat race.

Many parents have been their teens' assistants. They work tirelessly to ensure that their teenagers will compete: recruit tutors and private sports trainers and arrange for pricey SAT prep courses. They make it their obligation to help their children create transcripts that would please "big colleges." Moreover, they send a message that their children must succeed in all tasks to land a full scholarship in such a college.

5. Kids are not practicing emotional skills.

We stress academic readiness and make no effort to give children the emotional qualities they need to excel. A nationwide survey of first-year college students showed that 60% feel emotionally unprepared for college life. Knowing how to manage your time, battling depression, and taking care of your emotions are the main components of a healthy life. Without healthy coping strategies, it is no wonder teenagers feel stressed about their daily issues.

6. Parents see themselves as protectors rather than guides.

Somewhere down the line, the role of parents seems to have switched from guides to protectors. Now they have come to feel that their job is to help children grow up with few or no emotional and physical wounds as possible. They are so overprotective that their children never practiced coping with problems independently. Consequently, these children have grown up too emotionally frail to deal with life facts.

7. Adults do not understand how to help children confront their anxiety in the right way.

On the one hand, you will see parents who drive their children too hard. They push their children to do things that frighten them. On the other, are parents who do not pressure children at all. They let their children opt out of things that seem anxiety-provoking. Exposure is the only way to overcome anxiety, but only if it is achieved incrementally. Without preparation, subtle nudging, and encouragement, children never dare to face their fears head-on, and with sudden and over-exposure, children become scarred for life.

8. Parents are parenting from a place of shame and anxiety.

Parenting stirs up painful feelings, such as remorse and anxiety. However, instead of encouraging themselves to express these feelings, more parents are modifying their parental patterns. So they do not let their children out of their sight, and it stirs up their anxieties, or they feel so bad for saying no to their children that they back down and give in. As a result, they teach their children that uncomfortable feelings are unbearable.

9. Kids do not have enough free time to just be kids.

While structured sports and clubs play an important part in children's lives, adults make and enforce the rules. Unstructured play teaches children essential lessons, such as how to handle disputes without adult referees. Moreover, solo play shows children how to be alone and be relaxed within their own skin.

10. Over-attachment to familial hierarchies.

Although children give the impression that they would like to be in charge, deep down, they know they cannot make the right decisions. They expect their parents to be leaders—even where there is dissension in the ranks. Moreover, when the hierarchy is muddled—or even turned upside down—their fear skyrockets.

Chapter 3:
The differences between general anxiety and specific phobias

We all feel anxiety from time to time. Whether it is riding through turbulence, expecting a shot at the doctor's office, or living through a violent storm, fear is a common emotion that we have gone, are going, or will go through at some point in our lives.

However, if you have a particular phobia, you will likely feel fear or distress when confronted with that specific circumstance or object. A relevant phobia is a form of anxiety disorder described as severe or unreasonable fear or aversion of anything. These unfounded fears can interfere with personal relationships, work, and education and keep you from enjoying life.

Unlike Generalized Anxiety Disorder (GAD), there are several types of phobias. They are triggered when a person is faced with or even anticipates being confronted with a particular circumstance or object. Even if the circumstance or entity poses little or no immediate risk to the person, they cannot control their fear of it and deliberately avoid it at all costs. While people with clear phobias understand the irrationality of their fears, the thought of these fears alone is sometimes enough to cause immense, crippling anxiety.

While ordinary fears cause less anxiety and can be resolved more quickly, specific phobias affect a person physically and/or mentally to such an overwhelming degree that they are detrimental to their everyday lives.

Types of Specific Phobia

Relevant Phobias can be classified into five types:

• Pet Phobias (e.g., dogs, snakes, or spiders)

• Phobias about the natural world (e.g., heights, storms, water)

• Blood-Injection-Injury Phobias (e.g., fear of seeing blood, receiving a blood test or shot, watching television shows that display medical procedures)

• Phobias of being unable to escape (e.g., airplanes, elevators, being in a moving vehicle, enclosed places)

• Other phobias (e.g., phobic avoidance of situations that may lead to choking, vomiting, or contracting an illness; in children, avoidance of loud sounds like balloons popping or costumed characters like clowns)

Causes of Phobias

In most cases, particular phobias arise in early childhood between the ages of 7 and 11, while others can develop at any age. Several factors may cause relevant phobias, including experiencing a traumatic incident (e.g., being bitten by a dog); seeing someone experience a traumatic event (e.g., watching an automobile accident); a sudden panic disorder (e.g., traveling in a plane); or informative communication (e.g., extensive media coverage of a terrorist attack).

Sometimes, people who have a particular phobia cannot recognize the cause that their phobia. Although the cause of a specific phobia may be unclear, it is important to consider the signs and note that phobias can be treated if you seek treatment from a qualified mental health provider.

Factors of vulnerability

The risk factors for the emergence of a particular phobia are temperamental, environmental, and genetic. For example, negative affectivity (a tendency to experience negative feelings such as disgust, frustration, apprehension, or guilt) or behavioral avoidance are temperamental risk factors for several anxiety disorders, including particular phobias. Parental overprotectiveness, physical and sexual violence, and stressful experiences are examples of environmental risk factors that increase a person's probability of having a particular phobia.

There may also be an inherited vulnerability to a particular type of phobia; for example, if a person has an immediate relative with a specific situational phobia of flight, the individual is more likely to experience the same phobia than a phobia in any other category.

Symptoms with Specific Phobia

Physical Symptom:

- Racing of the heart;
- Difficulty in breathing;
- Weeping or shaking;
- Sweating;
- Feeling nauseous;
- Experiencing dry mouth;
- Having chest pains or feeling tightness in the chest.

Emotional signs:

• Feeling overwhelming anxiety or fear;

• Recognizing that your anxiety is unfounded, but feeling unable to resolve it;

• Fear of lack of power;

• An overwhelming desire to run.

Diagnostic Criteria DSM-5

The 5th edition of the Diagnostic and Statistical Manual of Psychiatric Disorders (DSM-5) outlines seven diagnostic conditions for specific phobias:

• Marked concern or apprehension over a particular item or situation; (In children, fear or anxiety may be expressed by crying, tantrums, freezing, or clinging).

• A phobic item or condition nearly often triggers immediate panic or anxiety.

• A phobia-inducing item or condition shall be avoided or endured with extreme terror or anxiety.

• Panic or apprehension is out of proportion.

• Apprehension, Anxiety, or avoidance is chronic, usually lasting for six months or longer.

• Apprehension, Anxiety, or prevention induces clinically severe depression or disability in social, educational, or other critical aspects of functioning.

Disruption is best explained by manifestations of another psychiatric illness, including terror, anxiety, and avoiding circumstances consistent with panic-like symptoms or other incapacitating symptoms; artifacts or situations linked to obsessions; memories of stressful events; alienation from home or attachment figures; or social situations.

All of us have these, and they usually start in infancy. Although they become a phobic disorder—or known as a particular phobia—when the terror is too strong, and the fear of seeing a snake or a spider or a dark spot causes us to break down and renders us useless to work.

According to the DSM-5, prevalence rates are about 5% for girls, 16% for 13-to 17-year-olds, and around 3-5% for older persons. Females are more affected than males.

Social anxiety disorder (SAD) and generalized anxiety disorder (GAD)

While some substitutes have been made for the definition of anxiety disorders since the publishing of the 5th edition of the Diagnostic and Statistical Manual of Psychiatric Disorders (DSM-5 for short), social anxiety disorder (SAD) and generalized anxiety disorder (GAD) appear to coexist under the same diagnostic group. Even if they share similar traits, GAD and SAD (sometimes called social phobia) are distinct disorders.

Shared Features

Both GAD and SAD are characterized by chronic fear, which is severe or disproportionate to the real danger. However, the sense of "threat" varies between the two.

People with SAD often undergo physical signs associated with their anxiety, such as those with GAD. Biased thinking—in several cases, catastrophizing (imagining worst-case scenarios)—is key to all types of anxiety disorders.

GAD and SAD may both occur together, and any of these symptoms raises the risk that a person may develop depression or other anxiety disorders, such as obsessive-compulsive disorder.

Differences

While the forms of thought traps can be identical, it is the thought content that separates GAD from SAD. People with GAD appear to have a gazillion worries. These can be over big life issues—such as well-being or finances—and minor day-to-day concerns that others may view as trivial.

Among those with GAD, social problems are not rare. However, their attention and focus are on problems, whether big or small, real or imaginary, that occur in current partnerships and relationships rather than on the fear of how they measure up. For example, a person with GAD could be uncontrollably worried about the consequences of a fight with their spouse, whereas a person with SAD is concerned with what people think of them being together. A mother with GAD may be unnecessarily worried about whether she has made the right decision to make her child switch schools.

Individuals with social anxiety disorder, on the other hand, prefer to think about encountering, watching, and performing in front of strangers (for example, speaking up in class or playing an instrument before a crowd). Their thinking process appears to rely on negative judgment and likely dismissal.

For example, a person with a social anxiety disorder may have trouble initiating a conversation at happy-hour at work for fear that they might show their fear, say "something dumb," or be mocked by their peers. An individual with a social anxiety disorder may avoid dating because of anxiety about feeling humiliated or embarrassed on a date.

The common thread here, again, is the pathological level of concern that inhibits the individual's ability to establish or sustain relationships, meet essential responsibilities and fulfill his or her personal and professional obligations.

Although the other elements of the fear cycle—emotions and thoughts—overlap, it follows that the interpersonal variations in GAD and SAD are subtle. A high level of prevention is a characteristic of both disorders, but the cause for the prevention is likely to be different.

Let us presume a person makes a sick call on the day of a career presentation. If this person has GAD, they might avoid meeting out of fear that they have not made enough effort to schedule their talk, or the presentation isn't good enough, or will never finish in time. If this person has SAD, they may avoid meeting out of fear that no one might like their proposals or that someone would mind if they sweat during the presentation.

Developmental Questions

The "normal" age of occurrence for GAD's is more than that of social anxiety disorder, age 31 for the former and age 13 for the latter.

That said, people with GAD sometimes have symptoms even before they seek care.

Adolescence and early adult stressors, as people usually undergo multiple social changes (for example, colleges, friendships, or romantic relationships), can intensify social anxiety symptoms. Adult accountability (for example, investments, childcare, or job decisions) exacerbates GAD symptoms.

In older people, the cause of concern and associated actions may differ slightly. For example, older adults with social anxiety disorder can feel anxiety and discomfort over appearance or disability (e.g., impaired hearing or tremulous movements) that may discourage or significantly decrease social experiences.

Physical symptoms than psychological symptoms more easily characterize the most common presentation of GAD in older adults.

Later in life, individuals with GAD are more likely to have uncontrollable worries about family members' well-being.

Why Anxiety Disorders May Still Develop in Older Adults

It is not rare for people with GAD to follow the requirements for another medical disorder over their lifespan or simultaneously. Depression is the most prevalent co-occurring problem. However, a large number of individuals develop a co-occurring GAD and social anxiety disorder.

GAD and post-traumatic stress disorder (PTSD) also exist simultaneously.

Luckily, therapies for GAD and social Anxiety disorder differ. They can both be managed with the help of authorized prescriptions from your physician. Cognitive-behavioral psychotherapy is the front-line psychotherapy for these disorders. This therapy method allows to overcome biases in thought and remove as much detrimental behavior as possible.

Chapter 4:
The difference in Child anxiety and OCD

What is obsessive-compulsive disorder in children?

Obsessive-compulsive disorder (OCD) is also a form of anxiety disorder. Obsessions are persistent feelings. Compulsions are repetitive habits.

An OCD child has persistent feelings and repetitive habits that are not desired. When children grow up, habits and obsessive thinking generally happen for an age-based intent and concentration. Preschool kids also have schedules and habits when it comes to eating, washing, and going to bed. This helps to stabilize their hopes and perception of the future. School-aged children create social rituals while learning by playing games, engaging in team sports, and chanting rhymes. These routines help children socialize and learn to cope with fear.

When a child has OCD, intrusive thoughts and compulsive rituals may become very repetitive and strong. They can interfere with day-to-day living and normal growth. OCD is more common in teenagers.

What induces OCD in your child?

The cause of OCD is unclear. Research indicates that this is a brain problem. People with OCD do not have enough of the chemical known as serotonin in their brains.

OCD has a propensity to run in the family, so maybe it is inherited. However, it can also arise without an OCD family history. In some cases, streptococcal infections can cause or exacerbate OCD.

What are the indications of OCD in a child?

Each child exhibits different symptoms. Below are the most common ones:

• Intense fascination with soil or germs;

• Repeated queries as to whether or not the door is closed

• Insistent thoughts of abuse, injuring or killing someone, or harming oneself

• Spending long periods touching stuff, counting, and worrying about numbers and sequences

• Preoccupation with order, symmetry, or accuracy;

• Constant reflections about inappropriate sexual acts or practices considered taboo.

• Disturbed by feelings that are counter to personal moral values

• A great desire to know or recall stuff that may be very trivial

• Too much attention to detail;

• Too much thought about the negative happening

• Violent feelings, impulses, or actions

Compulsive behavior is a repeated ritual used to relieve the discomfort induced by obsessions. They can be excessive, time-consuming, and destructive. They interrupt everyday tasks and relationships. They may contain the following:

• Repeated hand-washing (about a 100 or more times a day)

- Checking and rechecking several times, such as making sure the door is locked

- Sticking to strict rules of order, such as placing clothes in the same order every day;

- Holding artifacts

- Numbering and recounting a great deal

- Sorting items or placing things in a particular order;

- Making mantras out of certain phrases;

- Ask the same questions again and again

- Making disrespectful (obscene) gestures;

- Repeating sounds, phrases, numbers, or music to oneself

The signs of OCD may tend to be closely related to other health conditions. Make your child visit a health care provider for a diagnosis.

Can an infant be born with OCD?

Yes, and a child psychiatrist or other mental health specialist can diagnose it. He or she will determine the child's mental health. To be diagnosed with OCD, the child should have chronic, extreme, and disruptive obsessions and compulsions.

How is OCD treated in the case of a child?

Treatment will depend on the diagnosis, age, and physical health of the child. It will also depend on how severe it is.

OCD therapy requires a variation of the following:

- **Therapy with cognitive and behavioral methods.** Cognitive approaches allow the child to recognize and understand his or her fears. They also teach a child new ways to help overcome or reduce their fears. Behavioral strategies enable children and their relatives to make pacts or rules to restrict or alter behavior. One example is setting the maximum number of times a compulsive hand-washer can wash his or her hands.
- **Family therapy.** Parents have an essential role to play in the recovery phase. Treatment can also be included in a child's education.
- **Selective serotonin reuptake inhibitors (SSRIs).** These drugs help increase the level of serotonin in the brain.
- **Antibiotics.** Your child may need these medications if his or her OCD is related to a streptococcal infection.
- Teens with OCD can also have some eating disorders and will require medication.

The Difference Between Child Anxiety and OCD

Anxiety and OCD can sound super similar, and it is important to distinguish between them because the methods of management differ widely.

When someone has anxiety, there is a greater chance of having OCD. Both Anxiety and OCD have a significant genetic aspect because if someone is genetically predisposed to anxiety, they might also be genetically predisposed to OCD.

Chapter 5:
Anxiety and social media

If there is one thing that the 21st century has brought more to our lives, it is the enterprise known as "social media." From apps like Facebook to Twitter, or more photo-oriented applications like Instagram, the way people communicate with each other has shifted and developed in ways that our grandparents and even our parents may never have expected in their youth. In years gone by, social encounters were mainly face-to-face interactions, with the occasional letter writing thrown in as a form of long-distance communication. Then the phone was invented, which reduced the number of face-to-face interactions, but because it was in "real-time," it required a level of social knowledge.

With the arrival of smartphones and their easy availability for the younger and younger populations, real-time encounters have become a thing of the past. Research has shown that one of the key reasons why texting and other types of social communication are superior, particularly in the case of those dealing with social anxieties, to real-time encounters, is that the awkward nature of in-person contact is replaced by a quick text that can be filtered and controlled before it is sent, allowing for more co-operation. Today, it is hard to see young people (and not so young people) using their cellphones to make calls. Text messaging has become the preferred mode of contact. However, even messaging is supplemented by other technological methods, such as the ever-popular "Snapchat," where photographs are transmitted instead of lines of text.

Social Media and Social Anxiety: Blessing or Burden?

Some researchers see social media as a medium for social engagement for those battling social anxiety.

However, for those struggling with social anxieties, where every interaction is monitored, the challenge of social media as either a benefit or a disadvantage becomes even more acute. For the nearly 15 million people across the country suffering from social anxiety, online experiences can be either beneficial or negative. Hofmann (2000, 2007) conceptualized social anxiety in three types.

The first group consists of attitudes about social contexts in which unreasonable priorities, expectations of social success, low social self-efficacy, and dysfunctional beliefs about the possibility and cost of acting having a poor effect on social experiences at all stages. In an online world, because communication is not in real-time in most situations, a person dealing with social anxiety has time to build and tailor a self-image in whatever form they want. Expectations for social success will make real-time interactions time-consuming for a person suffering from social anxiety. However, in an online conversation, those standards are fulfilled in a manner that is not possible offline.

Hofmann's second group spoke about how people who suffer from social anxieties have assumptions about poor self-perception, rumbling, and intensified self-focused attention. In an online world, people with social anxieties have time to process how they want to present what they mean. In real-time, handling the intricacy of social life often does not allow the same amount of time to process how one expresses oneself. Because those suffering from social anxiety focus on previous potential conversational faults, the online and social media platforms require careful portrayal of conversation, making ruminating more difficult for certain individuals. (Others, though, ponder over how much attention they want their posts to get relative to others, or how fast or slow people respond to their tweets, or whether they get an answer at all!)

The third group is the use of social media for people coping with social anxieties. It has a countervailing influence in that social media is seen as a method of preventing real-time encounters with individuals. A study (Koo, Woo, Yang, Kwon, 2015) shows that those who participate in online social activity see a higher degree of well-being than they often show in offline social activity. In essence, social media and the Internet, paired with encouragement to escape real-time experiences, are associated with heightened social anxiety.

Overall, this suggests that using anonymous social media driven by resisting real-time social interaction does not change the propensity for automatic sensitivity and vulnerability to perceived self-image challenges encountered by those dealing with social anxieties. Social media and the Internet make it easier to alter and exploit social experiences, thereby allowing the "ideal self" to be conveyed to others. This difference between the "actual self" that cannot be changed before being introduced in a social setting, and the "ideal self" that can be modified before being presented, may lead to a decline in well-being. It is often considered that the level of engagement on social media could be devalued when it is generally viewed to be based on inflated and dishonest online self-presentation.

The ultimate conclusion is that the use of social media by people dealing with social anxiety as an alternative to face-to-face interactions results in weaker well-being and lower self-confidence if it is not combined with real-time engagement.

Chapter 6:
The link between anxiety and learning difficulties

Can Learning disorders, ADHD, and anxiety occur together?

Yes, they could. Evidence shows that children with intellectual disorders and/or ADHD are more likely to encounter cognitive and emotional problems. Here are some instances of this.

Some difficulties involving low academic performance make children feel as if they are not as good as their peers. This may affect their self-esteem and may worsen anxiety if preventive factors are not put in place. Protective factors can include such aspects as loving parents, close social relations, and extracurricular activities.

Some research literature reports that symptoms of ADHD can precede anxiety and vice versa if they are not treated. For example, a child with ADHD can have trouble interpreting social cues, recognizing body language, and have difficulty coordinating social activities that may lead to a child feeling uncomfortable or insecure in social settings. If this pattern persists, an anxiety disorder will develop.

A child with Learning Disorder or ADHD may have persistent problems reaching deadlines or finishing assignments, leading to feelings of nervousness if these trends persist.

Research shows that children with LD or ADHD can also have poorer working memory capabilities. Working memory is the capacity to retain information in your head, work with it somehow, and recall when needed. Sometimes, working memory is considered the "post-it paper" of the brain. Challenges with working memory may affect the person's capacity to plan, solve problems, and control themselves. This can make it problematic for people to navigate and adapt to their environments.

ADHD and anxiety impair memory functioning in several ways. Anxiety and ADHD make it impossible to ignore irrelevant stimuli. For example, due to the fear-based aspect of anxiety, individuals are often more focused on the concern; that is, thoughts are tainted with threats. On the other hand, it is generally more difficult for people with ADHD to ignore irrelevant stimuli such as sight and sound. In all cases, Anxiety and ADHD use the child's working memory capacity, limiting the child's ability to retrieve information. This may have an adverse impact on academic performance and work.

Reason for anxiety and stress in a child with a Learning disorder and ADHD

Children with learning disabilities may be more susceptible to anxiety and depression than others for a variety of reasons:

- Processing deficits can make life feel stressful. The familiar is comfortable, but the unfamiliar is a nightmare for certain children.
- For a child with LD/ADHD, going to a restaurant can feel like a young child in Times Square on New Year's Eve: too many people, too much noise, and the sense of being stuck can lead to fear. The next time the kid is supposed to leave, he starts to panic hours before. By the time he can go, he expects the worst and would rather sit where he feels safe than move into the

unknown. Since no one else knows why he is so angry or acknowledges his discomfort, the effect is that he feels lonely.
- Frequent feelings of shame and humiliation in school can cause emotional problems. Think of what it sounds like to be a girl with dyslexia who wants to write an in-class article about the book she has been reading. Maybe her book was a little less advanced than the other kids, or she could not finish it. She realizes that her spelling and punctuation would be full of errors and that the possibility that she will generate a cohesive class essay is slim to zero. She feels humiliated, weakened by her challenges, inefficient, and severely depressed.
- Biological mechanisms such as brain transmitter dysfunction or a family history of depression or anxiety may also precipitate these problems. Cortisol is a hormone that spontaneously enhances the body's development during periods of stress. It is responsible for the "fight or flight" reaction, encouraging people to either face an aggressor or escape. Increased depression and anxiety may be associated with elevated cortisol levels when a child is overwhelmed.

Anxiety disorder in autism

Anxiety disorder has consistently been shown to be associated with intellectual disorders as well as autism. Besides, it is proposed that the co-morbidity between autism and intellectual disabilities results in a higher risk of psychological conditions (Hill and Furniss, 2006; Bradley et al., 2004). Hill and Furniss (2006) indicate that people with autism and extreme intellectual disorders have greater levels of anxiety disorder than other non-autistic categories. This observation is consistent with Bradley et al. (2004), who have found that teenagers with autism and serious developmental disorders are more vulnerable to anxiety disorder.

Autism-specific co-morbidity can also make children and young adults with intellectual disabilities and autism more vulnerable to anxiety disorder. Many published studies to date directly look into the prevalence of anxiety disorder in children and young adults with mild to severe intellectual difficulties and autism. This research aimed to define the prevalence of anxiety disorder in children and young people with learning disabilities and autism.

The latest findings have found that there are more people suffering from anxiety disorders in the autism and LD community. According to Hill & Furniss (2006), people with extreme LD and autism are more worried about DASH-II subscale scores than people with similar levels of LD without autism. This is consistent with the Bradley et al. (2004) study, which compared psychological and behavioral problems in two classes of people with LD, one with an autism diagnosis and the other without, using DASH-II as a screening tool. The results for the autism community are correlated with a higher prevalence of mental health problems specific to anxiety disorders.

Individuals with autism spectrum disorders (ASD) have elevated anxiety disorders (Holt et al., 2004). Research by Kim et al. (2000) showed that high-functioning autistic children are at higher risk of anxiety than the general public, although the associations and risk factors for these particular issues remain uncertain.

In terms of how young people with moderate LD perceive fear, Wilson et al. (2005) indicate that people with LD did not discuss their perception of mental health problems in general terms but preferred to use specific terms frequently related to uncomfortable emotional and physical sensations. They used terms like temper, afraid, fed up, and 'stuff wrong with me' to describe clinical signs of anxiety and depression, such as sweaty palms and hyperventilation.

Why is it important to consider the variations that occur between these disorders?

To deliver successful and individualized care. It is necessary to consider the distinctions between LDs, ADHD, and Anxiety.

Learning Disabilities: Therapies for Learning Disabilities usually rely on clear and direct remedial training and classroom accommodation to promote academic success.

ADHD: Typical therapies for ADHD include the use of stimulant or non-stimulant drugs, as well as therapeutic interventions and parent instruction that do not target anxiety-related ill-adapted thought.

Anxiety: Anxiety therapies usually include anti-anxiety treatments and CBT exposure therapy and are not aimed at neurological disorders involved with ADHD.

Some useful methods for ADHD may not be effective for anxiety because what is effective for anxiety may not be effective for LDs, and vice versa.

Chapter 7:
Anxiety Explanation for Kids

Humans, like all animals, have self-protective systems to help us survive our flight, battle, or freeze survival reaction. The F F F, for short, is meant to prepare our brain and body to battle an opponent, run from an avalanche, or freeze to keep hidden from a predator. Our brain often misinterprets healthy conditions that are risky and may set off false alarms. When our brain, the amygdala, to be specific, feels the danger, our body enters survival mode faster than our conscious mind can respond by attempting to find out why we think we are in mortal danger. When the FFF alarm is blown, we start breathing harder and shallower, triggering hyperventilation leading to an increase in CO_2 in the blood. This causes dizziness or light-headedness, which many people perceive can make you faint, but only a sudden decrease in blood pressure causes fainting. The hearts start pounding very rapidly. These changes can induce extreme chest pressure, which many people perceive as signs of a heart attack when it is simply just the product of FFF stimulation, which can be relieved by breathing exercises as a way to get you ready for action. Blood is redirected to major muscles like that of the legs. Blood rushes out from our digestive system allowing the bladder to relax, and we may feel the urge to pee, the mouth goes dry, and we feel nausea. We get the butterflies sensation in our stomach. Blood often flows from the extremities leaving us with cold hands and sweaty palms. While the body begins sweating to stop overheating, legs and hands will tremble when tension hits. As our pupils get dilated, we get tunnel vision to improve our focus, but as a result, we lose our peripheral vision. FFF stimulation also decreases our capacity to detect changes in facial expressions from too much oxygen.

Depression disorder and elevated levels of stress have negatively affected the brain's ability to slow or cancel incorrect FFF activations, making it impossible to detect and mitigate their consequences by regularly recognizing the signs of false activations.

Due to lack of proper education, youngsters believe that their worries and complaints make sense or that they are warnings to be taken seriously. They generally assume that their level of fear is a true expression of how dangerous a situation is, instead of recognizing that their fear responds to anxious thoughts about a problem, like needing to solve a math puzzle, only parents can step in and re-label anxiety as only one line of thinking. Helping children know that anxiety is not the same as being in danger is an inspiring discovery. Just like how horror movies scare everyone but aren't real, kids will understand that one effective way to alleviate fear is to alter their mind's narration about the situation. When they are less scared, it would be easier to tackle activities and circumstances that have traditionally been avoided.

For young Child

Use stuffed animals to play the roles of the characters in your child's "horror" story, and introduce the "brave hero" who sweeps in to save the day.

For School-Aged Children and Teens

Have the child make two pairs of glasses, concern glasses and smart glasses, explain the condition by the various glasses and highlight the differences; Use the think bubbles to explain the "worry story" and the "smart story."

NOTES

PART 2

RECOGNIZING ANXIETY

Chapter 8:
Signs and Symptoms of Anxiety in Children

Please watch your child for these symptoms and visit your child's doctor if you find them daily. However, bear in mind that having one of these signs does not always mean that your child has an anxiety disorder. Your child's doctor would be more concerned about whether the signs will impair your child's everyday functioning or whether they will affect the rest of the family. For example, if math homework leads to a breakdown every night, or if it takes too long for your child to fall asleep, they are exhausted the next day and unable to attend school— these may be signs of an anxiety disorder.

Note, with that said, that fear does not just disappear on its own. Without medication, childhood anxiety will escalate and stimulate other severe mental health problems.

15 expressions to keep an ear out for

These sentences may be code words for "I am anxious":

"My stomach hurts." OR, "I feel like I am going to throw up."

Anxiety is in the body as much as it is in the mind. Stomachaches are very normal in nervous children since, in the throes of fear, the body redirects blood supply from the abdominal organs to the brain, which slows down digestion. This experience induces nausea.

"I am not very hungry."

When digestion shuts down due to fear, so does the urge to feed.

"Please do not let me do that." Or "Can I please stay home for today?" Or "I do not want to do that!"

Children with anxiety can begin to avoid stressful situations.

"Please do not leave me there." Or "Is it time to leave?" Or "I don't want to go back there."

Children with anxiety in a difficult atmosphere or circumstance will normally ask to leave to get away from the tension.

"I feel like I cannot do the right thing." Or, "I feel like something is wrong with me."

Kids with anxiety set impossible standards for themselves.

"I cannot do it!" Or "Will you do that for me?"

Anxious children demand perfection from themselves, so they avoid a challenging task to avoid making an error.

"I am so sorry."

Since nervous children are generally hard on themselves, they easily apologize, particularly for small things or even when they are not at fault.

"Are you upset with me?"

Many nervous children would seek continual approval or reassurance from others.

"I cannot go to sleep."

Children with anxiety may have trouble falling asleep.

"I feel so tired."

Kids with anxiety seem to have trouble falling asleep or finding restful sleep but complain incessantly about feeling exhausted.

"But what if, uh...? What if, uh...?"

The wheel in the brain of an anxious child is always turning, concocting worse-case scenarios.

"Nobody is going to fight for me." Or, "I do not have many friends."

Any child with anxiety has an extreme fear of social environments, particularly not being picked to join a team by their companions.

"Are you sure about that?" Or "Do you believe that?"

Kids with anxiety like to ask many questions to help relieve some of their fears, like, "Are you sure we are not running late?" Or "Do you think the teacher is going to like my science project?"

"I feel very hot." Or "I cannot breathe."

An anxiety attack (or more generally referred to as a panic attack) can cause hot flashes and sweating. Some signs of a panic attack include a racing heartbeat, trembling or sweating, shortness of breath, chest pain, dizziness, light-headedness, tingling, and chills.

"I have got a fever."

Anxiety or a panic attack will also induce headaches.

Watch these 15 Habits

The following actions can be symptoms of childhood anxiety. Although this list is not exhaustive, it lists the most common signs of childhood anxiety as gathered from various sources.

- Crys sometimes or sometimes feels unhappy.
- Is quick to anger
- Gets in a poor mood quickly or without a strong cause.
- Carries out acts that are sometimes irritable
- Appears to have trouble thinking or focusing.
- Gets terrified easily, often because of phobias or exaggerated fears.
- Awakens in the middle of the night screaming and crying because of bad sleep or nightmares.
- Undertakes actions in obsessive or compulsive ways, such as thinking about germs, organizing things in a certain manner, finger tapping, and so on
- Experiences of prolonged tantrums or meltdowns
- Turns down invitations to socialize with classmates.
- Appears to be too obsessed with their school grades.
- Overreacts to positive feedback from parents or teachers.
- Runs or hides to escape unpleasant circumstances
  Becomes clingy when they assume you leaving for a short while is an act of abandonment.

Chapter 9:
Identifying and Managing Fears, Worries, and Phobias

What is fear?

Fear is a reaction to a known or unknown threat. If you walk down a dark path, for example, and a person points a gun at you and shouts, "This is a robbery," you get frightened. The danger is actual, visible, and immediate. There is a strong and present object of terror.

While the emphasis of the reaction is different (real vs. perceived danger), fear and anxiety are interlinked. When faced with fear, most people feel the physical responses described in anxiety. Fear can induce anxiety, and anxiety can give worsen the feeling of fear. Although the subtle differences between the two give you a greater view of your symptoms which may be beneficial to your recovery plans.

What is worry?

Worry is a part of the symptoms of anxiety.

Anxiety has three main components: mental, biochemical, and cognitive.

Imagine that you have got a presentation coming up at work. You can note feelings of fear and dread; these constitute the emotional aspect. You can also experience physical symptoms, such as heart palpitations, sweating, or tightness in the stomach; these are physiological aspects.

Finally, you might say, "I cannot do it," or, "I am going to embarrass myself." Worries and pessimistic thinking form the cognitive aspect.

What are phobias?

Phobia is an intense and unreasonable response to anxiety. If you have a phobia, you can feel a profound sense of terror or panic when you confront or are confronted by the source of your fear. It may be of a certain location, certain circumstances, or some objects. Unlike common anxiety disorders, a phobia is typically related to something particular.

The effect of phobia can vary from irritating to seriously crippling. People with phobias also know that their paranoia is unfounded, but they cannot do anything about it. Such fears can interfere with work, education, and personal relationships.

Approximately 19 million Americans have a phobia that creates trouble in certain aspects of their lives. If you have an insecurity that keeps you from living your fullest life, visit your psychiatrist.

Causes of phobias

Genetic and environmental factors may induce phobias. Children who have a close family member with an anxiety disorder are at risk of having phobias. Distressing incidents, such as near-drowning, can lead to a phobia. Exposure to enclosed areas, heights, and bites of animals or insects may also cause phobias.

People with chronic medical problems or who have irrational worries over their health also have phobias. There is a high rate of people experiencing phobias following traumatic brain injury. Substance abuse and depression are also related to phobias.

Phobias have distinct symptoms than extreme psychiatric disorders such as schizophrenia. People experience sensory and auditory hallucinations, visions, anxiety, negative signs such as anhedonia, and disorganized symptoms of schizophrenia.

Social Phobia

Social phobia is often referred to as the disease of social anxiety. It is an intense fear of social circumstances which can contribute to self-isolation. Social phobia can be so severe that simple interactions, such as ordering at a restaurant or answering the phone, can induce fear. People with social phobia sometimes go out of their way to escape public environments.

Agoraphobia:

Agoraphobia is a fear of environments or circumstances from which you cannot run. The term itself refers to the "fear of open space." People with agoraphobia worry that they might be caught in big crowds or get stuck outside the house. They also avoid social environments and hide in their homes.

Many people with agoraphobia worry that they will have a panic attack in a place that they cannot run from. Those with serious health issues worry that they may experience a medical emergency in the public area and that there will be no assistance available.

Other forms of phobias

Glossophobia: It is known as performance anxiety or fear of speaking in front of a crowd. People with this phobia experience serious physical reactions anytime they think of standing in front of a group of people. Glossophobia therapies can include either rehabilitation or medicine.

Acrophobia: This is the fear of height. People with this phobia avoid cliffs, bridges, or the top floors of houses. Symptoms include dizziness, sweating, and feeling like they will go through or lose consciousness.

Claustrophobia: This is a dislike of confined or small spaces. Extreme claustrophobia can be particularly debilitating if it prohibits you from traveling in cars or planes.

Aviophobia: This is the fear of flight.

Dentophobia: Dentophobia is a dislike of dentistry or dental operations. This phobia usually occurs following a traumatic encounter in the dentist's office. It can be dangerous if it stops you from having the oral treatment you need.

Hemophobia: It is a phobia about blood. An individual with hemophobia can faint when they come into contact with their blood or the blood of another person.

Arachnophobia: that means fear of spiders.

Cynophobia: This is the fear of dogs.

Ophidiophobia: People with this phobia are terrified of snakes.

Nyctophobia: This is the fear of night or gloom. It almost always starts with a traditional childhood terror. When it progresses past puberty, it becomes a phobia.

Factors of vulnerability

People with an inherited predisposition to fear could be at high risk of developing phobias. Age, socio-economic class, ethnicity, and gender tend to be risk factors for some phobias. A typical example is the fear of animals; women are more likely to develop animal phobias. Children or individuals of poor socio-economic status are more likely to have social phobias. Men make up the bulk of people with the fear of dentists, doctors, and hospitals.

Symptoms of Phobias

A common reaction people experience when they come in contact with the object or cause of their phobia is a panic attack. The attributes of a panic attack include the following:

- Heart racing
- Speech slurring or failure to speak due to dry mouth
- Shortness of breath
- Upset stomach
- Nausea
- Increased blood pressure
- Shaking
- Pain in the chest or tightness
- An expression of shock
- Dizziness or light-headedness
- Sweating profusely
- A feeling of inevitable doom

However, a person with a phobia would not have to have a panic disorder for an appropriate diagnosis.

Choice for treatment

Phobic therapy can require rehabilitation strategies, drugs, or a mixture of both.

Cognitive behavior treatment

Cognitive-behavioral therapy (CBT) is the most widely used treatment for phobias. This includes sensitivity to the root of anxiety in a safe environment. This therapy will decondition people and reduce their anxiety.

The treatment centers on recognizing and modifying suicidal emotions, unhealthy attitudes, and negative responses people go through when they are confronted by their phobias. New CBT strategies use augmented reality technologies to introduce individuals to the origins of their phobias comfortably.

Medicines

Antidepressants and anti-anxiety treatments can help to calm the fear. A mixture of medicine and clinical counseling is always the most helpful.

Chapter 10:
Identifying and Managing Depression in your Child

About children's sadness and depression

It is common for children to feel sad, be cranky, or think negatively – this is part of normal learning and growth to controlling emotions. Yet childhood depression is more than just a gloomy, blue, or poor feeling.

Child depression is a mental health condition that affects children's thoughts, mood, and behavior. Children with depression frequently feel pessimistic about themselves, their condition, and their prospects.

When your child is sad, it will be hard for your child to understand, make friends, and make the best of everyday life. If depression continues for a long time without medication, children will fall behind at school, lose trust in themselves and withdraw into themselves, a cocoon, so to speak.

Children with the right treatment will rebound from depression. Your love and care still play a significant role in helping your child to heal.

When your child hints at thoughts of suicide or self-harm – like "I wish I were dead" or "I do not want to wake up anymore" – you should take them seriously. Get psychiatric support right away from your GP or ring the toll-free, confidential suicide helpline—+1 800 273 8255.

Signs of children's depression

If you found any of the symptoms to be stated in your infant and they lasted more than two weeks, your child could have depression.

Changes in your child's feelings or actions

You might find that your child looks depressed or upset most of the time, is aggressive, does not do what you ask most of the time, or has many temper tantrums.

Says bad stuff about themselves – for example, "I am not good at something" or "No one at school likes me."

Feels guilty – for example, your child might say, "It is always my fault."

Keeps saying that their tummy or head hurts, and they do not seem to have a physical or medical cause.

Changes in your child's participation in daily tasks

You might notice that your child does not have as much enthusiasm as they normally. They do not want to be with friends or hang out with the family, are not interested in playing or doing activities they used to love, have trouble sleeping, focusing, recalling things, or making clear choices.

Changes in your child's actions or academic success at school

If your child is in kindergarten, you may also find that your child does not do too well academically and has trouble fitting in or getting along with other children.

What to do if you are concerned about your children's depression

Depression does not go on its own. If you think they have depression, you need to support your kids.

Here is what you ought to do:

See the General Physician (GP) or Family physician and get a referral to a pediatrician, psychiatrist, or psychologist who can diagnose depression in infants.

If your child has difficulty discussing with you how they feel, you may want to inquire if they wish to speak to another trustworthy adult. But please let your kid know that you are there for them and want to know what is going on.

By seeking early support for your child with depression, you can help your child get well faster, decrease the likelihood that your child will experience depression later in life, and help your child grow up well.

Your GP will also speak to you about ways to handle your child's mental welfare.

Kid depression management: clinical assistance

Your child's psychologist or therapist can use cognitive behavioral therapy (CBT) to help your child improve unhelpful or unhealthy mental patterns and behavior.

Your child's therapist can use other methods, such as yoga, parent therapy, play therapy, or family therapy, to assist and encourage your child to learn to think more positively and cope with challenges. This means that your child will be less likely to develop depression again.

Think of yourself and your child's health providers as a team. Speak to experts on ways to improve your child's treatment at home.

Kid depression management: assistance at home

As well as engaging with mental health providers, here are some easy and efficient ways to support your child:

Take time to speak to your kid and listen to their thoughts. You might do this by sharing dinner or going for a stroll.

Gently urge your child to engage in activities they usually enjoy when they feel sad; this takes their mind off of what is bothering them.

Manage the tension and stress of your kids. Daily family activities that allow time for fitness, recreation, and socializing with friends will help. Having a night of adequate sleep will also reduce the child's stress.

Look for help materials to help your child practice relaxing techniques, such as deep breathing, gradual muscle calming, imagination, and mindfulness.

Speak to your child's teacher or school psychologist to find the right ways to help your child in school.

If your brothers and sisters and other family members realize that your child has depression, they can support you by acknowledging and caring. But before you tell anyone, ask your child if it is okay. Your child must permit you to inform others.

Take care of yourself when your child has depression.

If your kid has depression, it is not your fault.

It can be very painful for you to see your child feel angry, depressed, or be distant for a long time. In families, the way one person thinks and reacts may influence other family members.

While it is easy to focus on taking care of your kids, it is important to take care of your health and well-being. Start finding psychological support for yourself if your social life is disrupted by depression and worry. Your GP is the right person to talk to.

If you are physically and mentally well, you will be better able to take care of your kids.

Speaking to other parents can also be an excellent way to seek advice. You can interact with other parents by joining a face-to-face or online parent support network in related cases.

Chapter 11:
Identifying Social Anxiety

Social anxiety disorder is often confused with the shyness of family members, peers, and students, but it is a lot more than that.

Everyday social experiences can be frustrating for teenagers with social anxiety disorder. They may be unnecessarily worried about being ashamed, insulted, judged or disqualified, or upsetting people in social settings.

These doubts and worries can become overwhelming, leading young people to fall behind in academic and developmental terms. Children and teenagers with social anxiety disorder are much more likely to experience depression and drug dependence than those without.

That is why healthcare providers need to recognize the mental and physical signs of social anxiety disorder early.

What is social anxiety disorder, and how prevalent is it in adolescents?

Social anxiety disorder is a chronic and unreasonable fear of a social situation. Exposure to new individuals may be especially anxiety-provoking; however, people with social anxiety disorder can often be unable to communicate with or appear in front of others who are strangers to them. Although anyone, irrespective of age, can develop social anxiety disorder, it rarely does after 25 years. The onset time is typically in late childhood and adolescence.

Social anxiety disorder and its types

The fifth(5th) edition of the Diagnostic and Statistical Manual of Psychiatric Disorders (DSM-V) recognizes two subtypes of social anxiety disorder:

Generalized disease with social anxiety: Characterized by constant and crippling fears in most social environments, events, and relationships.

Non-generalized social anxiety disorder: characterized by debilitating apprehension of certain forms of social contact or behavior, in particular, performing before a crowd (e.g., giving a speech, speaking in front of a group, performing an act in public, etc.).

Prevalence in the U.S.

According to the National Comorbidity Survey Teen Supplement's screening interview results, an estimated 9.1% of teenagers, 13-18 years of age, in the United States reported social anxiety disorder at the time of the survey. The data also showed that social anxiety disorder was more prevalent in females (11.2%) than males (7.0%). Approximate 1.3 % of teenagers have serious impairments.

Social anxiety- typical symptoms in teenagers

Asking someone out on a date, presenting in front of a class, or performing in front of others are understandably nerve-racking experiences. It is not rare for teenagers to get uncomfortable in such social settings.

However, for teenagers with social anxiety disorder, these and other conditions and behaviors can cause fear. Teens with social anxiety can show intense nervousness around peers or teammates. They usually:

- Avoid eye contact

- Avoid social gatherings and meetings
- Sit alone at lunch
- Become anxious and awkward with others.
- Feel very nervous about meeting new people.
- Make up reasons to skip such social circumstances or activities.

Physical signs and symptoms of social anxiety can include:

- Rapid pulse
- Hyperventilating
- Sweating
- Shaking
- Pain in the stomach or nausea
- Mind becomes blank
- Difficulty in breathing
- Dizziness or light-headedness
- Tension of the muscle

Teens with social anxiety disorder frequently fear social situations such as going to parties, forming groups, or attending a school dance. They may have an excessive number of school absences. Entry to a classroom where students are already seated leads to intense self-consciousness. They might stop dating or not date at all, and using a public bathroom can be very inconvenient.

Undiagnosed and misdiagnosed social anxiety disorder

American society seeks to foster and reward extraversion and gregariousness. Despite this, parents of children with social anxiety disorder can underestimate or are oblivious to their child's fears and anxieties regarding social situations. They may associate their child's reluctance in social settings with "shyness" or believe that, since their child rarely acts out or gets into trouble, he or she is automatically self-disciplined.

It is important to distinguish between shyness and social anxiety. Although shy children can be more cautious about meeting others or talking in a group, they also interact with other children and adults, but with less enthusiasm than their peers. Shy children normally do not get upset when they have to communicate with others, whereas children with social anxiety disorder get upset and terrified by those interactions.

Identifying the warning sign of social anxiety disorder

Social anxiety may manifest as selective mutism (fear of speaking to others outside the immediate family or near friends). In grade school, children will avoid engaging in groups such as Girl Scouts or Little League. In middle school, social gatherings and extracurricular sports may be discouraged, and in high school, they may be isolated and frustrated, which may lead to academic difficulties and substance use.

Parents can help keep social anxiety from getting worse by looking for the following warning signs:

- Discomfort in talking to colleagues, coaches, and others
- Blushing, shaking, or defensive body language around other people
- Tantrums or screaming when approached by unfamiliar people (especially young children)
- Avoids making eye contact

- Talks softly or mumbles when approached by someone.
- Complaints of stomach aches or headaches to stay at home as opposed to going to classes, field trips, or social activities
- Signs of depression or use of Drugs (especially teens)

Parents who notice these symptoms should contact a family specialist as soon as possible to determine their child's diagnosis.

Since social anxiety disorder entails panic and anxiety that interfere with everyday schedules, education, work, and other activities. It is crucial for health care/mental health providers, educators, and parents to be able to recognize signs of social anxiety disorder so that teenagers get the treatment they need early in life.

Social anxiety treatment

Care for social anxiety disorder typically requires a mixture of therapy and medicine.

Exposure therapy is also used in the process of recovery. It requires a gradual introduction to awkward social conditions until the individual feels relaxed in such situations. Exposure therapy operates by "reconnecting" the brain's anxiety reaction to social circumstances. Relaxation therapy, including deep breathing and meditation, can also be beneficial.

The FDA has approved specific drugs for depression and anxiety to treat social anxiety disorder. These include Paxil and Zoloft selective serotonin reuptake inhibitors (SSRIs) and Effexor selective serotonin and norepinephrine inhibitors (SNRIs). These drugs should be used with care in children, at the discretion of the doctor, since they can induce side effects, including headache, stomach discomfort, nausea, sleep disorders, among others.

Beta-blockers (usually used to treat elevated blood pressure or heart problems) are especially helpful for certain people suffering from this disorder.

Possible long-term effects of social anxiety

Social anxiety in children can become a long-term disability, such as underemployment and the risk of depression and drug misuse. It may also lead to loneliness, weak coping skills, low self-esteem, and suicide or suicide attempts. Children suffering from social anxiety can suffer from depression. Parents and students need to be able to understand the symptoms of social anxiety disorder.

How schools/teachers can support students with this disorder.

Schools and individual instructors can better assist students with social anxiety disorder by providing an atmosphere in which students can express themselves easily.

Wherever possible, student support workers can collaborate with socially nervous students on guided exposures at school, such as accompanying them to the cafeteria to start discussions, buy food, or to the library to ask the librarian some questions. Connecting a student with an understanding peer friend to accompany on a social experience will also help.

Chapter 12:
Identifying Separation Anxiety

The term "separation anxiety" is mainly found in early childhood. When children grow more conscious of their environments and continue to grasp the environment around them, they struggle to distinguish themselves from caregivers. A toddler who has moved to a nanny or a daycare environment yells and cries as the caregiver leaves. While painful for the caregiver to observe, this aspect of childhood growth is reasonably normal, and there are ways to facilitate these changes.

What parents do not often prepare for is a resurgence of separation anxiety in "big kids." All school-aged children and teenagers may be dealing with separation anxiety and, in some cases, may grow into separation anxiety disorder. According to the Diagnostic and Predictive Manual of Psychiatric Disorders, Separation Anxiety Disorder is seen in 4 % of children and 1.6 % of teenagers, making it the most prevalent anxiety disorder in kids below the age of 12. Although a few drop-off and post-school cries are reasonably typical in children and do not raise red flags, the signs of Separation Anxiety Disorder can cause concern. Rejection of schooling, sleep disruption, and unnecessary anxiety, when faced with separation, will adversely affect the day-to-day living of an infant.

Symptoms of Separation Anxiety

The hallmark characteristic of Separation Anxiety Disorder is intense apprehension or anxiety over separation from home. This fear or anxiety exceeds what is expected of the person due to their stage of growth.

Children and teenagers with Separation Anxiety Disorder have at least three of the following symptoms:

- Recurrent extreme anxiety when expecting to or leaving home
- Persistent and unreasonable concern about missing the attachment figure or potential harm to them due to sickness, injury, tragedy, or death
- Refusal to leave home for school or to perform other tasks and events out of fear of separation.
- Excessive fear of being alone
- Refusal to sleep away from home or sleep without being close to the person you are emotionally attached to (attachment figure).
- Nightmares on separation
- Medical symptoms like headaches, stomach aches, and/or vomiting while away from attachment figures.

Separation Anxiety Disorder in children and teens lasts for at least four weeks and causes extreme depression. Separation Anxiety Disorder can also affect social interactions and family relationships.

Treatment of Separation Anxiety

There are many therapies widely used for Separation Anxiety Disorder. The faster you act to seek clinical support for children and teenagers, the faster your child will most likely achieve the desired result in therapy.

Having a psychotherapist who works with children and teens is the first step towards helping your child cope. Various forms of psychotherapy could be effective in treating Separation Anxiety Disorder.

Cognitive Behavioral Therapy (CBT) is the best type of psychotherapy recommended to treat Separation Anxiety Disorder. Via CBT, children learn how to understand their nervous emotions and bodily reactions to anxious thoughts. They learn to understand their problems and the habits of thinking that lead to their uneasy feelings. Using several approaches, children develop ways to control their nervous thoughts and feelings and deal with their emotions.

Family counseling

Bringing parents and other family members into the recovery process will increase the chances of positive outcomes for the infant. In family counseling, parents and siblings may discover new ways to communicate with the infant and figure out behavioral habits. They will also learn useful techniques to help the kid out with their anxieties.

Play-Therapy

Younger children can have trouble differentiating between ideas, emotions, and behavior. Play therapy can help these children demonstrate and process their feelings and learn to deal with them.

Relaxation therapy is important for children and teenagers who are dealing with Separation Anxiety Disorder. Deep breathing, directed relaxation, and gradual muscle relaxation will also help children and teenagers learn to be calm during an uncomfortable period.

Many children and teens appear to exhibit signs of Separation Anxiety Disorder even after therapy. If symptoms continue to adversely affect your child and make it difficult for your child to attend classes or even leave the house, medications can help. It is necessary to obtain a drug assessment from a child and adolescent doctor, as drugs may have serious side effects for children.

How do parents support children at home?

There are few suggestions that parents should follow to help children and teenagers learn to control their nervous emotions. Parental guidance plays a vital role in helping children learn to cope individually. Use these techniques at home to help your child excel outside the home:

- Create a schedule to help your child move to a school in the morning (come early, serve as a teacher's assistant before the other children arrive, exercise on the playground before the bell rings)
- Help your child reframe anxious thoughts by putting together a list of optimistic thoughts (it even helps to write these on cards to put in the child's backpack)
- Write comments on a regular lunchbox that contain constructive phrases.
- Avoid overscheduling—emphasis on playtime, downtime, and good sleeping habits.
- Warn your child to make adjustments to routine ahead of time.
- Empathize with your child and praise how far they've come.

Chapter 13:
Identifying Low self Esteem

It is easy to shrug off low self-esteem as a personality trait or to confuse it with humility. However, low self-esteem has long-term harmful effects, ranging from minor– not speaking up in class or at work meetings, for example – to major effects, such as relationship problems or self-harming behaviors.

Identifying the signs of low self-esteem is a critical first step in building trust; the next step is to determine your value. Here is how to get started.

Nine signs of low self-esteem

How often do you stop talking because you are afraid of embarrassment or being wrong? Do you often say "I am sorry" when it clearly isn't your fault?

These small self-confidence "blips" can sum up and lower your self-esteem. There are nine signs that you need to be aware of so you can start treating it (with a therapist or life coach):

1. Difficulty in speaking up and overfocusing on the needs, desires, and feelings of others.

2. Saying "I am sorry" and/or feeling bad for everyday interactions

Feeling sorry over stuff like taking up space; sorry for something you have no influence over or responsibility for.

3. Not "rocking the boat."

A tendency to follow what others are doing, saying, wearing, and going where they go.

4. Not feeling deserving or capable of getting "more."

This can lead to unfulfilled (or even toxic) partnerships, unsatisfactory or low-paying work, and generally lower expectations.

5. Difficulty making your own choices and having trouble standing by them after making them.

6. The lack of proper boundaries, which could lead to vulnerability and self-harm.

7. Doing things or buying gifts excessively for others.

Even for those who would not appreciate it, to feel wanted, needed, or seen

8. Negative self-Image

You do not think people would like or accept you for who you are.

9. Critical, abusive internal dialog

Talking harshly to yourself and perpetuating negative self-talk

Ten ways to build trust and self-confidence

You should work on building and rebuilding your self-esteem! By focusing on your self-esteem, you will feel even more comfortable with yourself and bond with your responsibility and pleasure.

1. Seek professional help.

Going to self-esteem therapy can help you identify and understand the origin of low self-esteem.

2. Prioritize a workout that feels good for your body. Even minor doses of activity, such as yoga, can improve your brain's serotonin levels and help you feel calmer, help you make healthier decisions, feel safer, and feel more in control of yourself.

3. Put your health first with a well-rounded meal.

There is a strong mind-body relationship, so when we feel healthy physically, it can dramatically impact our self-esteem and how we feel emotionally.

4. Get a list of your priorities or objectives.

Make it a routine to outline your goals every day, week, or month. Try to stick to them to get rid of other people's needs, demands, and requests.

5. Pause and evaluate before automatically saying "yes" to the request.

Just ask yourself: Am I saying yes because this is something I want to do, or just because this person likes me/needs me/approves of me?

6. Get started uplifting yourself!

Leave some questions or love notes to yourself around your home, office, car, or any other space you spend time in. "I am beautiful, and I have full confidence in myself; I am successful and worthy," for example. (Because it is you). Soon, these assertions will not feel foreign to you – and you will begin to feel it and believe it!

7. Start meditating, using positive affirmations.

There are a lot of free apps you can choose from, like ThinkUp and Shine.

8. Notice and try to limit comparing yourself to others.

Ask yourself and think wisely; why does it matter so much to me what this person is doing/saying/wearing? A solid way to minimize this is to reduce social media exposure.

9. Find your favorite way to relax and treat yourself.

This is a wonderful way to endow in yourself your self-worth.

10. Replace "I am sorry" with more situationally appropriate interjections.

Such as "Excuse me" or "Please beg your pardon," if necessary.

Or, depending on the situation, replace "thank you" with "thank you so much for your patience" when you are running late.

Chapter 14:
Identifying Stress

What is the Stress?

Stress is a sense of being under tremendous pressure, where this pressure outweighs the available personal and social assets. This strain can result from day-to-day tasks such as increased workload, a dispute, or an impending deadline. This form of stress is known as acute stress. Due to too many responsibilities, people who go through acute stress, too much anxiety, or weak organization may experience episodic stress symptoms, such as irritability. The most dangerous form of stress is persistent stress that affects a person for a long period. Chronic stress may significantly affect physical well-being, such as poor immune systems, digestive and intestinal problems, or mental health, such as depression. Early diagnosis and management are important in the prevention of long-term harm to the body and mind.

Source of stress

People respond differently to stressful circumstances, and what is stressful for one person may not be for another. All types of circumstances will lead to tension; the most prevalent are work, finances, and relationships.

Popular major life events that can cause stress include:

- Lack of Facilities at work
- Unemployment concerns
- Personal conflicts
- Illnesses

- Going back home
- Divorce

Some more frequently recorded sources of stress include:

- Arguments with family members or partners
- Feeling undervalued at work.
- Pressure of work
- Fatigue
- Driving in heavy traffic
- Uncertainty

These stressors will deplete our energy and make us more vulnerable to harmful stress-related symptoms. Mental health problems such as depression and anxiety can also make people feel depressed more quickly. However, often there is no identifiable cause.

Symptoms

Everyone feels stress, and although stress affects everyone differently, some general signs and symptoms need to be observed:

Psychological signs

- Inability to concentrate or make simple decisions
- Memory lapses
- Becoming rather vague
- Easily get distracted
- Less intuitive & creative
- Undue worrying/racing thoughts

- Feeling overwhelmed, unmotivated, or unfocused
- Depression and anxiety
- Negative thinking
- Insomnia or waking up tired
- Prone to accidents

Emotional signs

- Tearful
- Irritable
- Mood swings
- Extra sensitive to criticism
- Defensive
- Feeling out of control
- Lack of motivation
- Anger
- Frustration
- Lack of confidence
- Lack of self-esteem

Physical signs

- Aches/pains & muscle tension/grinding teeth
- Frequent colds/infections

- Allergies/rashes/skin irritations
- Constipation/diarrhoea/IBS
- Weight loss or gain
- Indigestion/heartburn/ulcers
- Hyperventilating/lump in the throat
- Dizziness/palpitations
- Nervousness or shaking uncontrollably
- Panic attacks/nausea
- Cold or sweaty hands and feet
- Physical tiredness
- Menstrual changes/loss of libido/sexual problems
- Heart problems/high blood pressure

Behavioral signs

- No time for relaxation or pleasurable activities
- Prone to accidents, forgetfulness
- Increased reliance on alcohol, smoking, caffeine, recreational or illegal drugs
- Becoming a workaholic
- Poor time management and/or poor standards of work
- Absenteeism
- Self-neglect/change in appearance

- Social withdrawal
- Relationship problems
- Aggressive/anger outbursts
- Nervousness
- Uncharacteristically lying

Strategies for self-management

There are various ways you can take to handle the tension individually, such as:

- Daily physical activity
- Reducing smoking, narcotics, and caffeine consumption
- Developing support networks
- Eating good
- Taking the time to rest
- Being mindful
- Having a restful night

Apart from incorporating self-help strategies, evidence suggests that the mere act of perceiving a demand as something we can manage and even improve decreases the strength of the stress response and encourages long-term well-being.

These symptoms tend to affect day-to-day functioning and remain present for an extended period where a psychiatric intervention can be placed in effect. Cognitive Behavioural Therapy and Mindfulness-based approaches are evidence-based approaches to stress reduction.

Chapter 15:
Managing Frequent Nightmares

Not every dream is pleasant; many are upsetting or even scary. Unpleasant dreams—especially ones that are disturbing or profoundly upsetting—are referred to as "nightmares," and most people have them from time to time. Any mental health condition and stressful life experiences can make someone more likely to have frequent nightmares. Getting frightening nightmares night after night interrupts sleep and eventually reduces the quality of life.

Understanding the Nightmare

Nightmares, while unsettling, are a common phenomenon for the vast majority of people. In dreams, nightmares often include characters, places, or other aspects of an individual's daily life that are rendered warped, scary, or otherwise unpleasant; like dreams, they are theorized to help people interpret memories or cope with uncomfortable emotions in waking lives.

Nightmares may be highly expected to occur when a person is depressed, nervous, or dealing with other stressful feelings in everyday life; they may also seem spontaneous. In certain cases, mental health problems can be caused (or exacerbated) by nightmares.

What triggers nightmares?

According to the DSM, nightmares are usually caused by fear or stress, trauma or upset, sleep disorders, a fluctuating sleep schedule, or prescription or substance use.

Are nightmares attributed to psychiatric illness?

Yes, in some situations. Chronic dreams have been associated with depression, dementia, PTSD, and some psychological disorders, such as borderline personality disorder. Some experts suggest that determining the occurrence and nature of nightmares can help physicians evaluate the development and seriousness of mental health disorders; increasingly regular death dreams, for example, may reveal the existence of suicidal thoughts.

Are nightmares a symptom of PTSD?

Yes, almost half of people diagnosed with PTSD reported have flashbacks after a stressful experience. Post-traumatic dreams include vivid memories of the traumatic experience itself, but they are not always there; others have themes. Irrespective of the themes, nightmares are associated with more extreme symptoms overall; on the other hand, targeting recovery nightmares has been shown to improve all symptoms.

What are the night terrors?

The term "night terrors" refers to a sleep disorder in which the person screams, cries, or even seems to be overwhelmed by extreme fear during sleep; the individual can even flail wildly or even wander about. Although night terrors can be very disturbing for family members or other observers, it is possible that the person who experienced them may not remember the incident in the morning. Night terror is a natural part of growth for many children; it is slightly less frequent in adults but is encountered by about 2% of adults.

Are nightmares and sleep terrors the same thing?

No, no. Night terrors entail physical movement and screaming and typically occur during non-REM(Rapid Eye Movement) sleep; since they happen in a deeper, slow-wave period of sleep, after waking up, the person will usually have no recollection of what happened. Nightmares are unpleasant hallucinations that occur during REM sleep. Screaming, thrashing, and other types of violent acts are not usual during nightmares. Also, since they occur during REM sleep (when brain function is highest), the person may typically have an idea of the nightmare when they wake up.

Nightmares Management

Nightmares that occur only rarely are also not a cause of alarm. But recurring dreams may suggest a major problem—such as stress or trauma—or may interfere with well-being by disturbing sleep or causing daytime anxiety.

Fortunately, there are various methods for managing nightmares, ranging from self-help (i.e., pre-bed calming techniques) to better sleep care to structured counseling. If repeated dreams unexpectedly appear without a discernible psychological reason, it may be wise to speak to a doctor; certain drugs or medical conditions, such as sleep apnea, may induce recurring nightmares.

How can you stop having nightmares?

The first way to start is by improving sleep hygiene, keeping to a more regular sleep schedule, engaging in a calming bedtime routine, reducing caffeine and alcohol, and exercising regularly to alleviate nightmares. The next step is to discuss the problem with a psychiatrist to decide if the dreams had any medical causes.

How do I decide where to get psychological when I have recurring nightmares?

If no medical triggers are known, some forms of psychotherapy— including cognitive behavioral therapy and vision reversal therapy— effectively minimize the incidence of dreams by helping a person navigate stress, fear, or depression that may be responsible for a bad dream.

Could medications be used to treat nightmares?

Yes, treatments used to treat PTSD, depression, or anxiety have also demonstrated some effectiveness in managing nightmares. Your doctor can recommend any potential drugs for nightmares, including olanzapine, clonidine, trazodone, and tricyclic antidepressants.

Can some foods trigger nightmares?

Many people claim that consuming some foods— such as dairy products or spicy foods— too near to bedtime can be a source of nightmares. Some study has found a correlation between self-reported eating patterns and nightmares, but researchers note that such findings should be viewed with caution. If it is likely that specific foods can induce digestive distress or affect one's mood—and may contribute to nightmares as a result—it may also be the result of confirmation bias or mere coincidence.

Lifestyle modifications and home remedies

If nightmares are a concern for you or your kids, consider the following strategies:

Set up a daily, soothing routine before bedtime. It is necessary to provide a regular bedtime routine. Do calm, relaxing activities—such as reading novels, solving puzzles, or bathing in a warm bath—before bedtime. Meditation, deep breathing, or calming techniques can also aid. Also, keep the bedroom cozy and peaceful for sleeping.

Give assurance. When your child is dealing with nightmares, be gentle, relaxed, and calm. When your child wakes up from a nightmare, act rapidly and soothe your child at their bedside. This could prevent any nightmares.

Ask your child to explain the nightmare. "What happened to you? Who was in a dream? What made it frightening?" Then tell your child that nightmares cannot harm them.

Imagine a happy ending to the nightmare. For your kid, you might urge him or her to "take a picture" of the nightmare, to "speak" to the characters in the nightmare, or to write about the nightmare in a diary. Sometimes a small amount of imagination can help.

If you have a problem with depression or anxiety, talk about it. Do any basic stress management exercise, such as deep breathing or relaxing. A mental health specialist will assist, if necessary.

Teach relaxation techniques to your child. Your child may feel more secure if he or she sleeps with a favorite stuffed toy, blanket, or other comfort items. Keep the child's door open at night, so he or she doesn't feel alone. Keep your door open, too, if your child wants to join you in bed at any point in the night.

Use the light of the night. Hold the night light in your child's bed. When your child wakes up at night, the light can be comforting.

NOTES

PART 3

OVERCOMING ANXIETY

Chapter 16:
Managing Your Anxiety While Raising Anxious Kids

Anxiety is part of human nature, and often the term "anxiety" is watered down. People are worried about a wide range of problems. Finance, work security, marriages, child-rearing, health, and safety come to mind as common daily concerns. Not all of them, however, qualify as fear.

One of the questions that parents frequently pose is, "Does my fear trigger anxiety in my children?" Research reveals that anxiety has a hereditary basis. Genetic tests indicate a 30-67 % heritability range for anxiety disorders. When a mother has an anxiety condition, there is a risk that the child may also have anxiety during his or her lifespan.

The other topic that needs to be considered: Can fear be catching? Well, it turns out, fear is not just a genetic matter. Parents and children may influence each other's nervous behavior by living together. Research conducted in the American Journal of Psychiatry looked at almost 900 households with adult twins who have children to assess the environmental impact on anxiety. The results showed good evidence for the ecological transfer of anxiety from parent to infant regardless of genetics. Essentially, this research has demonstrated that nervous behavior can be acquired and that an anxious child's behavior can also exacerbate a worried parent's behavior. The good news from this study is that parents play an important role in mitigating their child's anxiety by modifying their behavior and modeling appropriate coping strategies.

Watch out for these potentially nervous habits in your family:

Anxiety Talk

Children are attentive listeners and masterful eavesdroppers at all the wrong moments. You might find yourself repeating the same instructions over and over but to no avail, but the moment your kids tune in is precisely the time when you are having a private conversation with another adult.

It is important to process nervous feelings with someone who can listen and help you work through them, but it is equally important to remember that kids seem to fill in blanks when they hear little bits of potentially frightening material. Talking about your thoughts of a school shooting with your peers is healthy; talking about this topic in front of or near your children will heighten your fears and concerns.

Children watch their parents' doubts, fears, and nervousness speak and may internalize these thoughts.

Avoidance of Behaviors

If particular situations trigger fear in you, you can react by avoiding them. You might also follow this up by constantly explaining the root of terror. If, for example, you run away from dogs, you may also remember the time that a dog attacked you as a child to justify why you see dogs as unpredictable. This is a typical response to fear based on prior experience. The problem with this is that children soak up the actions of their parents and emulate them. In this situation, the message is that all dogs are frightening and unpredictable, and need to be avoided. To stop passing on your fears to your children, use the assistance of your partner or another adult in their life to make sure that your children have a safe response to your causes without the alarm center going off. In the event of anxiety over a dog, your partner may take your children to a pet day to look around.

Shielding Behavior

Negative parenting behaviors that cause anxiety may involve actions that try to protect children from any possible injury. Frequent reminders to be vigilant when playing and to set restrictions on how far children can climb or where they can leap are ways of protecting children during play. The point here is very clear: playing is risky, and you are going to get injured.

Kids need to partake in positive risk-taking to learn and understand how to make healthy choices. When parents protect children from possible risks that do not currently occur, they become risk-averse.

Parents can limit the environmental transmission of nervous behavior by taking the following steps:

Get to know your triggers.

Keeping a trigger diary for your nervous thoughts will help you figure out what triggers you to feel anxious and when you may need help. Personal fears often cause anxiety, but they may also be triggered by some locations and activities, excessive tension levels, or communication with others.

When you feel nervous, look at what is going on, the time of day, and what you have been dreaming about or doing right before feeling the wave of anxious symptoms. You can then pinpoint the trigger points when you stop the trend.

Encourage health risks

When children strive to push themselves and assess their strengths and shortcomings on their terms, they learn how to succeed in this environment. If watching your kids scale, a rock wall activates your warning center, ask a neighbor to join you in the park so that you can take a short stroll anytime you feel nervous. If socializing in big crowds is uncomfortable for you, but you want your children to feel relaxed in groups, drop them off at gatherings, or give them to your spouse or another parent to take them out.

Kids need to be encouraged to take safe chances. You do not have to join them on a roller coaster, but you have to let them try it.

Talk about healthy coping skills.

At times, we all feel nervous, and growing up is not all fun and games. When parents model safe strategies for managing and coping with stress and anxiety, children understand that they should deal individually with their causes and stressors. By:

- Teaching deep breathing (in for four, hold for four, out for four)
- Using a mindfulness app to keep calm.
- Teaching incremental muscle relaxing to relieve muscle pain
- Taking a stroll together every day.
- Encouraging the reading of newspapers
- Creating a family worry box to get the stress out onto paper and into the box.

Are some of the healthy ways you can teach your child to cope.

Anxiety can influence anything from education and job to physical wellbeing, relationships, and beyond. Learning to recognize the triggers and discover the skills that work for you not only helps you handle your anxious thinking loop it also shows your kids that they should learn to deal with their triggers and work with the ups and downs that inevitably arise when in adulthood.

Chapter 17:
Specific communication skills for Parents

Communication is the fundamental building block of relationships. By contact, we communicate our emotions, feelings, and connections to one another. Developing strong communication skills is crucial to a stable relationship, whether with an adult, child, partner, or relative.

We have all had moments where (1) we have thought to have heard and understood, and we have all had experiences (2) where we have felt confused and overlooked. Usually, when we feel noticed, we are less frustrated, anxious, and more receptive to problem-solving than when we feel misunderstood. Feeling heard and understood often builds confidence and care among people.

The communication process is a two-way street.

For communication to happen, (1) there must be a sender—who conveys a message—and (2) a receiver—who receives and understands the message.

In good communication, the sender is transparent and correctly conveys the message he is attempting to deliver. The recipient also obviously understands the message.

Miscommunication happens if the sender does not receive a direct reply and/or the recipient does not recognize the sender's message. Some things can get in the way of effective communication.

For instance:

- When we assume that we know what people are thinking or that they might know what we are thinking.
- When we reflect on what we want to hear as others talk—instead of listening to them.
- When we raise other questions and issues that are not relevant to the subject at hand.
- When we believe that we know what is best for others and want to persuade them of that.

These things either hinder us from delivering a direct message or prevent us from getting a response from the other person.

It takes practice and effort to communicate properly.

It is not something that comes easily to any of us. Below are a few steps to a strong conversation. At first, these skills and methods can appear odd and uncomfortable. But if you stick with them, they are going to be normal with time. As an additional benefit, you can strengthen your contact with others (inside and outside your family).

Listening Carefully

Active listening is a way of paying attention to someone that lets them know that you are working to hear the message they are sending out.

Make sure your body language conveys to them that you are engaged in listening. You can make eye contact with them, tilt your body towards them, and smile while they speak to let them know that you are listening.

Listen to the content and the emotions behind the sentences. Do not just listen to the substance of what is being said. Listen to the emotion that the individual is attempting to express to you. Are they showing pleasure, sorrow, enthusiasm, or anger—either by words or body language?

Teaching Children to Communicate

Children need to understand how to articulate themselves properly and how to listen to others.

From the time infants begin to utter sounds, they learn how to speak. They learn how to attract the attention of people and how to get their message out. They also discover that communicating is a two-way mechanism.

Children learn their abilities from how we react to them and how we communicate with them.

We also need to show kids how to listen consciously.

The kid has to rely on the individual who speaks—to eliminate as many obstacles as possible. This could mean shutting off the TV, telling them to smile at you, or getting them in the same room so you can talk to them.

When we have their attention, we need to teach young people to pay attention.

Children benefit the most by engaging with us and having us interact with each other.

We need to make sure that we are strong role models and take the time to listen and carry across our messages.

Family Communication

With more people, there are more possibilities for communication—and more opportunities for confrontation.

- There is an incentive for one relationship when two parties are involved.
- There is an incentive for three relationships when three parties are involved.
- There are six potential partnerships of four and so on.
- It is hard to meet everyone's expectations all the time.

Compromise does not suggest a winner and a loser, but simply that a "new alternative" has been sought.

Generating "win/win options" encourages us to be innovative about finding solutions to problems—rather than relying on our interests or desires. To come up with "win/win options," family members need solid leadership skills.

Here are several ways to come up with a "win/win" solution:

- It is vital that all parties in dispute be included—even if this means calling a 10-minute "time out" so that people can calm down. (Set the kitchen timer, and let people race around the block—or find a similar positive approach to help people cool down.)
- Use neutral words. This means that family members should not name-call or pass judgment on the ideas or wishes of others.
- The request of each family member must be considered. The voice of each member needs to be heard.

- All have to use their active listening capabilities (as outlined above)
- Once everybody is validated and respected, the process will continue to generate alternative ways to overcome the dispute.
- The community should create as many new solutions as possible to the problem—focusing on how to solve the problem, not just how to satisfy one's own needs.
- Keep a list of all the solutions that are created.
- Some of the solutions may be stupid and scandalous. Humor makes us calm our thoughts and will help us remember what has been discussed.
- When all possible ideas have been developed, run over each proposal and address it. "Is that going to fix the problem? Should we do so? How hard or fast will this be to do?"
- The parties involved will decide on the best solution possible. If only two parties are interested, they must agree to a solution before the matter can be considered resolved.

Chapter 18:
Teaching Kids to Change Negative Thoughts to Positive

Children can be the worst judges of situations. They may get caught in negative thought habits that lead to depression, amplify their anxiety, or make unpleasant feelings feel overwhelming.

If your daughter has not been invited to a birthday party, for example, she concludes that everyone going to the party hates her. If she fails to remember a line in a school play, she insists on having ruined the whole show.

These pessimistic modes of thought are often unrealistic, but they may profoundly affect their attitudes, actions, and world views. Mental health researchers term them cognitive distortions—sometimes referred to as cognitive error, thought error, or thinking error.

Any degree of cognitive distortion is common. We all make mistakes in our reasoning. It's because that kind of thinking is chronic and ingrained that a child's social life is likely to have many different emotions. I've never seen someone living under the weight of some mental health condition that doesn't make processing mistakes often.

In cognitive-behavioral therapy (CBT), children are encouraged to recognize common cognitive distortions that make them feel worse. Here they are divided into 11 common categories.

1. All-or-Nothing to think about (also referred to as Black-and-White Thinking or Dichotomous Thinking)

What it is: seeing people in just two categories, because they're either good or evil, black or white, with no shades of gray. A widespread distortion that makes you think—and so feel—that if anything isn't all that you want, then it's none of what you want. It's also assuming that you ought to do better in everything—perfectionism—or that you've completely lost.

E.g., I didn't get my first choice of school, so my dreams for high school are completely shattered. Or: If I didn't get the A+, I'm going to be a loser.

2. Emotional rationale

It is to believe that it must be real when you sense something, even though there is no proof other than intuition.

For example, I feel sad because no one likes me. Or: I'm terrified to go to the elevator because elevators are scary places.

3. Over-generalization

It is taking one bad experience or information about a circumstance and making it a common pattern and reality of your whole life.

For example, this person didn't want to hang out with me. No one's just going to hang out with me! Or: I fucked up my experiment in chemistry today. I'm never going to get it right!

4. Labeling As it is: place a misleading mark on yourself – or someone else's – so that you no longer see the person under the label. When you put others in such a position, your comprehension becomes so static that there is no space for a wiggle to see yourself or another person differently.

For example, I fell trying to score the goal in soccer today. I am a terrible klutz. In that conversation, I didn't have anything to say. I'm completely uninteresting!

5. Fortune-Addressing

What it is: guessing something is going to turn out to be wrong. This can be a cynical way of looking at the future, and it can affect your behavior, making the case that you are trying to predict more likely to turn out to negative.

E.g., I know I'm going to do a horrible test (so you panic and perform less effectively on it). Or: If I reach out to this person, they won't want to speak to me or welcome me (so you don't reach out and take the opportunity to get in touch with someone you want to know better or get support from).

6. Reading minds

It is assuming that you know and appreciate what another person is thinking and that you're generally confident they're not reflecting well on you.

E.g., I'm talking, and the person I'm talking to doesn't seem to pay attention to it. They don't like me; I'm positive. (In truth, maybe they're either distracted or stressing out over something unrelated to you, and they're having a hard time concentrating on it.)

7. Catastrophication (also called Magnification)

What it is: take over a problem or something bad and blowing it out of proportion.

E.g., This party is going to be the most terrible experience ever!

Or: If I failed to get a base hit, I'm going to die of shame.

8. Seeing the positive (also called Minimizing)

It is taking something positive that has happened and diminishing it so that it doesn't count as a good thing about your life or experience. It rejects all arguments against our pessimistic opinion of ourselves or our position.

E.g., I did good on that one quiz, but I just got lucky. Or: This person said, "I love to hang out with you," but she's just kidding. She doesn't mean it.

9. Mental filter (also called Selective Abstraction)

It is to see just the negative instead of looking at all the good or neutral sides of the experience.

E.g., you write a paper for an instructor, and they send you a lot of good reviews, but you spelled someone's name incorrectly. All you can think about is the spelling mistake. Or, in a day, you have a lot of constructive talks and one in which you say something humiliating. In absolute horror, you concentrate solely on the humiliating comment you made, ignoring all your other social experiences.

10. Personalization

This means having to blame yourself for what is in your control and even take it negatively because it is not intended to be detrimental.

For example, if I hadn't asked too much of my parents, they would not have had a divorce. Or: How dare that guy step in front of me, that was so rude! (It was an innocent mistake when the individual didn't notice you and cut you off.)

11. Imperatives

What it is: to think about "shoulds" and "musts" (and "should not" and must not").

E.g., I should be able to give lectures in class without any anxiety. What the hell's wrong with me? (Of course, thinking this way, as well as feeling anxious, makes you much more nervous about speaking!)

How parents can support children

CBT helps children recognize, criticize, and eventually restructure their thinking so that they can live happier better-adapted lives. Taking the lead from CBT, parents may help children understand perceptual distortions and reduce their severity.

The easiest way to get started is with your emotional distortions. If you've studied the various styles, strive to recognize them in your thinking habits. E.g., if your child has anxiety, you personalize it, assume it's your fault, and then call yourself a "terrible parent.

I can't emphasize enough how necessary it is to notice cognitive distortions in a way that isn't judgmental. When you know how to find distortions in your mind, you're in a much better position to make someone else notice theirs. And be humble about spotting your own – call them out in a playful way when you notice them, and let your children call theirs out, too.

The aim is to model for your children that we all make misconceptions, and the process of acknowledging them and making corrections with levity and self-compassion is typically the best medication.

If your kid has many cognitive distortions – if their reasoning is static, their beliefs are chronically pessimistic, or their emotions are too high to focus on their thinking errors – it's time to ask experts for support. It's fantastic to work with your child to understand and recognize cognitive distortions – particularly as a complement to effective counseling – so a child with severe difficulties will need to be seen by a mental health provider.

Chapter 19:
Practical Strategies to Coping with Social Anxiety

Social Anxiety Disorder (SAD) can be improved in several ways. While medication is available and proven to be successful in treating SAD, it is estimated that only 25% of people with the condition will ever undergo treatment. Though not a substitute for psychiatric therapy, self-help is a valuable starting point for those who cannot otherwise be helped. The following self-help techniques for social anxiety disorder should be used to relieve symptoms.

The Social Copping

Recognizing social skills that could use a bit of practice and focusing on developing them could help deal with the feelings and reactions that come with social anxiety disorder.

Assertiveness

Many individuals with social anxiety disorder lack assertiveness and can benefit from learning to become more assertive by self-help techniques.

Practice becoming more assertive by expressing your desires in a confident and relaxed manner that acknowledges the needs of others. Usually, this takes the form of "I" sentences, such as "I feel hurt because you're not responding to my phone calls." Learning to say no is also a vital aspect of being assertive and a trait that most adults with social anxiety struggle with.

How to be more assertive when you've got SAD

Non-verbal communication

Improving your non-verbal communication skills is another area where you can use self-help tools if you're living with social anxiety.

Most people with social anxiety prefer to take a "closed-off" stance; you can do this without even knowing it. Learning how to have a confident stance (e.g., hands by your sides, strong eye contact) allows people to react favorably to you and helps you look more available.

Verbal Communications

Besides taking a confident body stance, learning how to start conversations, keeping them going, and listening attentively are the skills that you will need to improve by self-help techniques.

As an example, one fast trick for engaging a group of people in the discussion is to listen first and then make suggestions about what they're talking about. For instance, "Are you talking about the results of the election? I could not trust them either."

Expose yourself in as many ways as possible to improve your verbal speaking skills. Practice being a good listener, answering open-ended questions, and telling stories about yourself so that people can get to know you better.

How to Have an Easy Conversation When You Have SAD

Telling Others Your Social Anxiety

Your closest relatives and friends are likely to get an understanding of your social anxiety. If you wish to tell a particular person, send a note that you'd like to discuss something and schedule a time and a private place to chat.

If you are too anxious to articulate your condition, please give a rundown of what you've been feeling. It's best to express the symptoms so that the other party can have an idea of what you're going through.

Remember that social anxiety disorder is not widely known, and some may need more information to understand it.

Managing anxiety with Emotional strength

Fear and suicidal thoughts are two of the most important feelings when you have social anxieties. A couple of basic tactics will help you solve them.

Deep breathing

Having social anxiety suggests that you are likely to experience intense emotional responses in social settings. One way to reduce these nervous responses is to keep the body in a calm state. When your body is calm, your breathing is steady and normal, and your mind is free from negative emotions, making it easy to enjoy being with others.

You are likely to breathe faster in fear-provoking conditions, which, in fact, will make the other anxiety symptoms worse. Below are a few steps to control your nervous and shallow breathing.

How to do deep inhalation

- Count the number of breaths you take in a minute (count an inhale and exhale as one). Please take note of this amount. The average human would take between 10 and 12 breaths per minute.

- Just focus on your breathing. Inhale and exhale through the nose. Take a deep breath into your diaphragm instead of a shallow breath into your chest. Inhale for three seconds and exhale for three seconds (use a watch or clock with a second hand). When you exhale, think about "relaxing" and relieve tension in your muscles. Continue to breathe like this for 5 minutes.
- Count your breaths per minute again to see how the number has gone down.
- Practice this breathing exercise 4 times a day when you're in a calm state of mind.
- When you're in group settings, make sure you're breathing the way you've practiced. This way of breathing would become automatic with time.

Reducing Negative Thinking

If you live with social anxiety, you can misunderstand other people's remarks or facial gestures that lead to your emotional reactions.

There are two typical modes of thinking that may add to the anxiety.

- Mind-reading: You presume you know what other people are saying about you (e.g., "Everyone can see how anxious I am.").
- Personalizing: You believe that someone's action is related to you (e.g., "He seems bored, I shouldn't have invited him to this movie").

The ideas you've got are so automatic that you actually don't even know you're worried about them. Below are a few strategies to help manage your depressive emotions.

How to Reduce Negative Thinking

Think back to the latest social situation in which you were nervous. Write down what you were feeling before, during, and after the experience.

Ask yourself questions in order to challenge your pessimistic feelings. For example, if your automatic negative thinking was "People are yawning, they must think I'm boring," ask yourself, "Will there be another explanation?" In this scenario, the alternate thinking may be, "It really didn't have anything to do with me; they were just exhausted."

Try to note the automatic pessimistic feelings you have before, during, and after the social interactions; you confront and challenge them with alternatives.

Face Your Fears

Avoiding feared scenarios may minimize your emotional reactions in the short term, but it seriously restricts your life in the long run. In comparison, the number of things you dread is increasing as the fear becomes more common. On the other hand, the incremental adjustment to social environments will help to reduce the fear and the negative responses you have associated with them.

Below are several methods to tackle the issue of running from your fears.

- Identify the top 10 conditions you're avoiding.
- For each condition on the list, break it down into a sequence of steps that increase in complexity.
- Tell a funny story about yourself to a gathering of people you know well or have just met.

- Talk to a group of peers about your real view.
- Voice the real impression to a group of outsiders.
- Make a dinner toast for people you know well and those you don't know so well.
- Practice every step as long as you need before you move to the next step. If you feel discomfort, question the pessimistic thoughts and use the deep breathing method to calm.

Note that the exact list you make depends on your fears. For example, you may be more afraid to talk in front of people you know better than a crowd of strangers. In this scenario, the elements on the list will be reversed.

Day-to-Day Strategies

Below are a few tips to help you deal with social anxiety daily, either at work or at school.

- Arrive early enough that you can greet people one by one when they arrive.
- Make a list of questions for your instructor or boss, and begin with the least anxiety-provoking ones.
- Keep up with current affairs so that you can take part in small chats.
- Avoid the use of alcohol to suppress inhibitions because it has the opposite effect.
- Choose a career you're passionate about such that even the more difficult aspects of work in terms of your social anxiety can seem worth it.

- Make new friends by welcoming strangers, offering compliments, and beginning short conversations.
- Get daily exercise, eat nutritious foods, and avoid caffeine and sugar to reduce anxiety.

Mistakes to Avoid

There are many common errors that people commit as they attempt to resolve social anxiety by self-help interventions. Avoiding these pitfalls will ensure things go your way.

- Don't even attempt to suppress your fear. The more you see it as something horrible that has to be avoided, the more concentrated you will be on it, and the tougher it will be to mitigate it.
- Never consider social anxiety as a characteristic of personality. Although you could be an introvert or have a propensity to be shy, social anxiety disorder is a mental health condition that does not describe who you are. It's easy to conquer the fear and enjoy a life of fulfillment.
- Although there is some evidence that cannabidiol (CBD), an ingredient of marijuana, can be beneficial to social anxiety, there are also dangers associated with its use. When considering using this as a coping mechanism, make sure to properly weigh the costs and rewards.
- Don't take too long to get treatment from a mental health specialist. Although it can be enticing to believe you can handle all of this on your own, people also need counseling or treatment to properly overcome social anxiety.

With time, when you are relaxed, confront pessimistic feelings, and face feared scenarios, then you can find it easier to remain calm in challenging situations. However, if you still experience serious anxiety regularly, it is vital to contact a psychiatrist or a mental health specialist, as conventional treatments such as drugs or cognitive behavioral therapy might be advisable.

Chapter 20:
Practical Strategies to Coping with Separation Anxiety

What's separation anxiety?

It's normal for your young child to be anxious when you say goodbye. In early childhood, crying, tantrums, or clinginess—all the hallmarks of separation anxiety—are a positive response to separation and a normal stage of development. It may begin before the child's first birthday and may recur until the age of four. While the severity and timing of separation anxiety can vary greatly from child to child, it is important to note that a little concern about leaving mom or dad is common. With empathy and the right coping mechanisms, the child's worries can be relieved—and completely go away with.

However, certain children develop a separation disorder that doesn't go anywhere, even with the parent's best intentions. These children suffer a continuity or recurrence of extreme separation anxiety during their primary school years. Suppose separation anxiety is excessive enough to interfere with daily events, such as education and friendships, and lasts for months rather than days. In that case, it may be a symptom of a bigger problem: separation anxiety disorder.

How to ease "natural" separation anxiety

For children with normal separation anxiety, you may follow these steps to make the separation anxiety experience better.

- Practice isolation. Leave your infant with a caregiver for short stretches and short distances at first. When your child gets used to this, you will eventually leave for longer periods and over longer distances.

- Schedule to go away after your child has gone to sleep or eaten. Babies are more vulnerable to separation anxiety when they are exhausted or hungry.
- Develop a quick "goodbye" routine. Rituals are reassuring and can be as easy as a special gesture through a window or a goodbye kiss. Keep things short and quick.
- Leave with no fanfare. Tell your kid you're leaving and you're going to come back, then go—don't stop or make it a bigger deal than it is.
- Honor your promises. To develop your child's trust, it's vital to return at the time you promised.
- Get a consistent main caregiver with you. When you employ a caregiver, aim to retain them on a long-term career to prevent inconsistency.
- Minimize the creepy/scary TV shows. Your kid is less likely to be scared if the shows they watch are not frightening.
- And try not to give in. Reassure your child that they are just fine—defining clear boundaries will allow your child to adapt to separation.

Common reasons for separation anxiety disorder

Separation anxiety disorder happens when the infant feels unsafe in a way. Take note of anything that could have thrown your child's life out of control, making them feel threatened or disrupted their daily routine.

If you can identify the underlying cause—or causes—you'll be a step closer to supporting your kid overcome their challenges.

Common triggers of separation anxiety disorder in children are:

Change of surroundings. Changes in the environment, such as a new home, school, or daycare, can cause separation anxiety disorder.

Stress. Stressful circumstances, such as school switching, divorce, or the death of a loved one—including a pet—can lead to separation anxiety issues.

Insecure attachment to caregivers. While a stable bond of attachment means that your child feels secure, understood, and comfortable enough for optimum growth, an unstable one will lead to childhood issues such as separation anxiety.

An over-protective father. In certain cases, separation anxiety disorder may be a symptom of your depression or anxiety. Parents and children should not feed each other's anxieties and fears.

Anxiety or trauma separation?

If your child's separation anxiety disorder seems to have occurred overnight, the cause may be a stressful event rather than separation anxiety. While these two disorders can share symptoms, they are treated differently. By learning the impact of emotional stress on infants, you will help your child recover with the most appropriate therapy.

Helping a child with separation anxiety

None of us want to see our children in danger, so it might be instinctive to help your child escape the problems they're scared of. However, this would only increase your child's fear in the long run. Instead of wanting to prevent separation if possible, you should help your child fight separation disorder by taking action to make them feel safer. Providing a friendly home atmosphere will help your child feel more relaxed. And if your actions don't fix the issue entirely, your sympathy will only make it easier.

Listen to your child's emotions and value them. For a child who might still feel alienated because of their condition, the feeling of being listened to may have a strong calming effect.

Talk about the problem. Kids should be able to chat about their feelings with you. Be empathetic, but still tell your child—slowly—that they survived the last split.

Anticipate the uncertainty of separation. Be prepared for adjustment points that can trigger your child's distress, such as going to school or meeting with friends to play. If your child is more readily separated from one parent than the other, that parent should be responsible for dropping off the child.

Keep cool during the separation process. If your kid sees that you can be calm, they're much more likely to be too.

Support the interest of the child in extracurricular activities. These are perfect ways to relieve their fear and help your child form friendships.

Praise the efforts of your kids. Use the smallest of achievements—going to bed without a fuss, a decent performance from school—as an excuse to compliment your child as a way to boost morale.

Suggestions to make your child feel safe and happy

Please have a clear schedule for the day. Routines provide children with a sense of confidence and begin to minimize their fear of the unknown. Try to follow mealtime, bedtime, and the like. If your family's timetable is going to be adjusted, talk to your child ahead of time. Change is good for children if it's anticipated.

Set the boundaries. Let your child know that even though you understand their emotions, there are rules in your home that need to be followed. Like schedules, setting and following boundaries lets your child know what to expect from any situation.

Offer options to your child. If your child has a preference or a degree of influence over their relationship with you, they will feel safer and more relaxed. For example, you might give your child a choice as to whether they want to be dropped off at school or what toy they want to take with them to daycare.

Simple separation anxiety disorder: school tips

For children with separation anxiety disorder, entering school can appear daunting, and a failure to go is commonplace. However, by discussing the underlying reasons for your child to delay schooling and making adjustments at school, you can help reduce your child's symptoms.

Help the kid who has been missing from school get back as soon as possible. And if a shortened school day is required initially to appease the child's worry until they learn that they will survive the split, then enforce that.

Ask the school to adjust your child's late arrival. If the school can be tolerant about late attendance at first, it can allow you and your child a little space to chat and develop at your child's speed.

Identify a safe spot for your child. Find the spot where your child should go to school to relieve fear during difficult times. Create instructions for the proper use of the safe spot.

Send your child notes to read. You should insert a message for your child in his or her lunch box or locker. A brief "I love you!" on a napkin will comfort the child.

Assist your child in encounters with peers. Adult assistance, whether by a teacher or a psychologist, can help both your child and the other children understand with whom they communicate.

Reward the actions of your kids. Just as at home, any positive effort—or little step in the right direction—is to be celebrated.

Help your child to relieve their stress.

Children of nervous or depressed parents can be more vulnerable to separation anxiety. To help your child relieve the effects of fear, you may need to take action to feel calmer and more focused.

Expressing what you're going through can be cathartic, particularly when there's nothing you can do to change the unpleasant circumstance.

Exercise daily. Physical exercise plays a vital part in the reduction and prevention of stress.

Eat well. A well-nourished body is well suited to deal with tension, so eat lots of fruit, vegetables, and good fat, and strive to resist unhealthy foods, sugary drinks, and processed carbs.

You can regulate stress levels with calming exercises such as yoga, deep breathing, or meditation.

Get enough sleep. Feeling exhausted only deepens your depression, making you act irrationally or foggily while sleeping well directly boosts your mood and increases productivity in your waking life.

Keep your sense of humor. As well as improving your outlook, smiling helps your body combat tension in a multitude of ways.

Whether to get medical assistance

Your patience and know-how will go a long way to supporting your child with separation anxiety disorder. However, certain children with separation anxiety disorder may require clinical intervention. To determine if you need assistance with your child, check for "red flags" or severe symptoms that go beyond milder warning signs. This includes the following:

- Age-inappropriate clinginess or tantrums.
- Removal from colleagues, families, or peers.
- Concern over excessive anxiety or remorse.
- Constant symptoms of physical illness.
- Refusal to go to school for weeks.
- Excessive fear of leaving home.

If the attempts to reduce these symptoms do not succeed, it might be time to see a psychologist. Remember, these may also be signs of a trauma that your child has undergone. It is critical to see a child trauma doctor if this is the case.

Treatment of separation anxiety disorder in kids

Child psychologists, Child psychiatrists, or pediatric neurologists can identify and treat separation anxiety disorder. These qualified physicians incorporate evidence from the home, school, and at least one professional visit to make a diagnosis. Keep in mind that children with separation anxiety disorder may have physical complaints that may need to be professionally assessed.

Specialists may treat physical signs, recognize anxious feelings, help the child develop coping skills, and promote problem-solving. Professional treatment for separation anxiety disorder can include: talking therapy. Talk counseling is a supportive and safe space for your child to share his or her emotions. Having someone listen empathically and guide your child to consider their fear has been proven to be incredibly beneficial.

Play counseling- The constructive use of play is a natural and beneficial way for children to learn about their emotions.

Counseling with the family- Family therapy will help your child counteract feelings that feed their fear, while you, as an adult, can help your child develop coping skills.

School-based advice- This will help the child with separation anxiety disorder explore the classroom's emotional, mental, and cognitive needs.

Medicine- Medications can be used to treat acute forms of separation anxiety disorder or can only be used in combination with other treatments.

Chapter 21:
Practical Strategies to Coping with Fear of Public Speaking

Glossophobia – fear of speaking in public. It's the single most common phobia. About 75% of people are diagnosed with it, self and/or medically diagnosed.

You're not alone in your panic. You can't cure the anxiety. However, you can control and reduce it.

WAYS TO MANAGE THE ANXIETY OF PUBLIC SPEAKING

Getting Ready

- Choose a topic of concern to you.
- Prepare carefully—know your stuff.
- Practice – rehearse your speech with a friend.

Get to know the audience.

- Challenge cynical thinking—make 3-5 cards of optimistic thinking, or have friends pen inspiring words about you.
- Expect favorable reactions—expect success!
- Know the room—if you're new, visit your speaking space before D-day.
- Employ aerobic exercise strategies—daily aerobic exercise can reduce anxiety by 50%.

- Eat for success—foods including tryptophan (dairy products, turkey, salmon) and complex carbohydrates help calm the body down. Remove coffee, sweets, and hollow calories.
- Sleep for success—know and get the number of hours of sleep you need for optimum results.

On the Day of Presentation

- Eat a few hours before the talk – not right before.
- Dress for success; your success! Dress comfortably and in a manner suitable to the case. Look your best
- Challenge bad thoughts– Continue constructive thinking
- If you need to, talk to a counselor about your worries.
- Review 3-5 inspiring thinking cards
- Practice your speech one more time
- Go to the room early to get ready with the machines and on the podium.
- Exercise right before talking to reduce the amount of adrenaline.

Employ anxiety-reduction strategies

- Aerobic exercises
- Relaxation of the deep muscle
- Visualization strategy
- Deep, rhythmic breathing
- Use the toilet right before the presentation.
- Take a sip of water before you speak
- Interpret the signs of anxiety as enthusiasm

- Use the podium to apply grounding — to stand still and remind yourself that you are firmly bound to the ground that is solid and stable under your feet.
- Use resources to reduce the audience's attention to you, such as:
  - Presentation of PowerPoint
  - Video movie clips
  - Handouts for
  - "Show and say" objects to be passed.
- Engage the crowd.
- Look for the friendly faces in the crowd.
- Use comedy when necessary.
- Use the free space of the room to your advantage–walk around as necessary.
- Adjust the speech appropriately.
- Speak clearly–enunciate.
- If possible, slow down.

Additional thoughts

- Seek public speaking opportunities to desensitize (reduce) the fear.
- Consider the use of anti-anxiety drugs.
- Gain experience–practice as much as you can.

Chapter 22:
Phrases for calming your anxious Child

It happens to every child in one way or another—anxiety. As parents, we would be keen to protect our children from the anxious times of life, but navigating fear is a vital life skill that will serve them in the years to come. In the heat of the moment, try these simple sentences to help your children recognize, embrace, and work through their tense times.

1. "Can you make it up?"

Drawing, sketching, or doodling their fear gives children a way out of their thoughts because they can't use their vocabulary.

2. "I love you. You're secure here."

It is a strong assertion to assure your child that they will be held protected by the one they love the most. Remember, fear makes children feel as if their brains and bodies are in danger. Repeating that they are healthy, safe, and loved will soothe their nervousness.

3. "Let's just imagine that we're blowing up a huge balloon. We're going to take a deep breath and blast it up on the count of five."

If you tell a kid to take a deep breath amid a heart attack, they're likely to say, "I can't!" Instead, make this a game. Pretend to blow up a balloon, make strange sounds in the process. Taking three deep breaths and blowing them out would help counteract the tension in your child's body.

4. "I'm going to say something, and I want you to say it just like I do, 'I can do it.'" Do this 10 times at different volumes.

Marathon runners use this trick all the time to get over the "wall."

5. "Why do you believe it is?"

This is mostly useful for older children who can better explain the "Why" of what they feel.

6. "What's going to happen next?"

When your children are nervous over a situation, help them work through the event and find out what will happen after that. Anxiety triggers a myopic vision, which makes life seem to fade after the incident.

7. "We're an invincible band."

Separation is a powerful cause of fear for young children. Reassure them that you're going to work together, even though they can't see you.

8. Get a battle cry, "I am a warrior!"; "I am unstoppable!"; or "Look out, world, here I come!"

There's a reason why movies show characters scream before going to war. The physical act of shouting balances anxiety with endorphins and reduces stress.

9. "If you're feeling like a demon, what does it look like?"

10. "I can't wait until _____."

Excitement about a coming moment is contagious.

11. "How about putting your worry on the shelf while we _____ (listen to your preferred song, run around the block, examine this story). Then we'll pick it back up again."

Those who are anxiety-prone frequently sense that they have to put their nervousness above all else. This is especially difficult when your kids are nervous about something they cannot change. Setting it aside to do something for enjoyment can help put their worries into perspective.

12. "This feeling will go away. Let's get comfy till it does."

The act of getting relaxed calms the mind and the body. Heavy blankets have even been shown to reduce anxiousness by way of increasing slight bodily stimuli.

13. "Let's talk some more about it."

Let your teens explore their fears by way of asking as many questions as they need. After all, knowledge is power.

14. "Let's depend _____."

This distraction method requires no preparation. Counting the number of sporting boots, the variety of watches, the number of kids, or the range of hats in the room requires commentary and thought, each of which detracts from the nervousness your child is feeling.

15. "I want you to count down from 160 seconds."

Time is a powerful device when young people are anxious. By observing a clock or the watch's movement, a child has a center of attention other than what is happening.

16. "Close your eyes now. Picture this..."

Visualization is a powerful tool used to relieve pain and anxiety. Guide your child into the imagination of a healthy, warm, peaceful place where they feel relaxed. If they listen intently, the emotional signs of fear will dissipate.

17. "Sometimes I get frightened. It's no fun at all."

Empathy wins in many, many situations. You could also strike a dialogue with your older child about how you overcame fear.

18. "Let's get out of our calm checklist."

Anxiety will hijack the rational brain; carry a checklist of your child's abilities. When the need arises, proceed with this checklist.

19. "You're not alone in the way you believe and feel."

Pointing out all the others who can express their worries and anxieties lets the child realize that resolving concerns is universal.

20. "Tell me the worst thing that might happen."

Once you've considered the worst-case scenario of your worry, ask about the possibility of the worst possible thing occurring. Then, ask your child for the best possible result. Ask them, finally, about the most probable outcome. This exercise aims to help the child think more calmly during his or her nervous experience.

21. "Working is helpful, occasionally."

This is counter-intuitive to teach to a child who is still nervous, but pointing out why fear is helpful reassures the children that there is nothing wrong with them.

22. "What does the bubble of your thought say?"

If your kids read comics, they're familiar with the clouds of thinking and how they move the plot forward. When learning about their thoughts as listeners or third parties, they will obtain insight into them.

23. "Let's find some proof."

Collecting data to confirm or deny your child's anxiety lets your children see if their concerns are founded on facts or not.

24. "Let's hold a discussion here."

Older children particularly enjoy this practice when they are allowed to argue with their parents. You could learn a lot about their logic in the process.

25. "What's the first piece we need to talk about?"

Anxiety also makes mountains out of molehills. One of the most efficient methods to overcome fear is to slash the hill down into small pieces. In doing this, we know that the whole experience is not creating a mountain of fear, just one or two small "rocks" of it.

26. "Let's mention all the ones you love."

Anais Nin is attributed with the quote, "Anxiety is the greatest murderer of love." If that assertion is valid, then love is indeed the biggest killer of anxiety; remembering all the people your child loves and why they love him will replace fear.

27. "Remember when you..."

Competence creates confidence. Confidence drives away anxiety. Helping the children remember a moment when they overcome fear gives them a sense of competence and trust in their skills.

28. "I am already proud of you."

Knowing that you are pleased with their efforts, regardless of the result, reduces the pressure to do something perfectly – a cause of frustration for many kids.

29. "We're going for a tour."

Exercise relieves discomfort for up to a few hours as it consumes extra fat, loosens stressed muscles, and increases the feeling of contentment. If your kids can't walk right now, get them to run around, bounce on a yoga mat, jump rope, or stretch.

30. "Let's watch the thought drive by."

Ask your children to imagine that the fearful feeling is a train that has stopped at the platform above their head. In a few moments, like all trains, the idea will move on to its next stop.

31. "Take a deep breath."

Model a soothing approach and inspire your child to look at you. If your children let you, hug them against your chest so that they can hear the sound of your steady heartbeat.

32. "How can I help you?"

Let your children lead the situation and tell you what kind of coping technique or tool they want in a particular situation.

33. "This feeling is going to fade."

Sometimes, children can believe that their fear is never-ending. Remind them that help is on the way instead of ignoring or squashing the worry.

34. "Let's put this tension ball together."

When the children turn their fear into a stress ball, they experience emotional relaxation. Make your handmade tension ball by filling a ball with flour or rice.

35. "I see the Widdle is nervous again. Let's teach Widdle not to think about it."

Create a character that represents a concern, such as Widdle the Worrier. Tell your child that Widdle is concerned and that you need to show him some coping skills.

36. "This is hard, I know."

Recognize that the situation is complicated. Your validation reveals that you love your children.

37. "I have a gift with the fragrance you love right here."

A scent mate, a fragrance necklace, or a diffuser will relax your anxiety, particularly when you fill it with lavender, sage, chamomile, sandalwood, or jasmine.

38. "Tell me about that."

Listen to the kids chat about what's bothering them without interrupting them. Talking about it will allow your children time to process their feelings and come up with a plan that works for them.

39. "You're so courageous!"

Affirm the willingness of your children to deal with the crisis, and this inspires them to excel.

40. "What kind of relaxing technique do you want to use right now?"

Allow the children to pick the soothing approach they want to use.

Chapter 23:
Learning to manage Worries

How to Avoid Anxiety

Are you overcome with endless worry and nervous thoughts? These tips will help you relax your worried mind and relieve your fear.

How much is too much to think about?

Worries, fears, and anxieties are a natural part of your life. It is normal to fret about an overdue bill, a forthcoming work interview, or a first date. Yet, "natural" concern becomes excessive when it is constant and uncontrollable. You obsess about "what ifs" and worst-case situations every day; you cannot get nervous thoughts out of your mind, and it interferes with your everyday life.

Constantly stressing, cynical thoughts, and constantly predicting the worst will take a toll on your mental and physical wellbeing. It will soak up your emotional power, make you feel nervous and jumpy, induce insomnia, headaches, stomach pains, and muscle pain, making it difficult to focus at work or school. Chronic anxiety is a significant symptom of Generalized Anxiety Disorder (GAD), a widespread anxiety disorder that includes stress, nervousness, and a general sense of unease that colors your whole life gray.

If you are afflicted with exaggerated anxiety and stress, there are steps you should take to toggle off anxious feelings. Chronic anxiety is a behavioral habit that can be tamed. It would be best to teach the brain to be calm and look at things from a more balanced, less fearful viewpoint.

How to Avoid Anxiety

Tip 1: Create a "worry" time every day.

It is hard to be involved in your day-to-day tasks when fear and worry dominate your mind and distract you from work, school, or home life. Rather than trying to delay or get rid of an anxious feeling, permit yourself to be so, then set off living with it until later.

Create a "concerned time." Choose a set time and place to think around. It can be the same every day (e.g., in the living room from 5:00 a.m. to 5:20 p.m.) and early enough not to make you nervous right before bedtime. During your time of concern, you are encouraged to worry over something on your mind. The rest of the day, though, is an anxiety-free time.

Write down some of your concerns. If you have an anxious thought or concern in your mind throughout the day, make a short note of it and then resume the day. Remember that you will have time to think about it later, so there is no reason to do so right now. Often, writing down your thoughts—on a pad or your phone or computer—is a lot more work than just worrying about them because your fears are more likely to lose their control.

Go down your "worry list" at your time for worrying. If the feelings you wrote down are still troubling you, encourage yourself to obsess about them, but only for the amount of time you have allocated for your time of concern. When you think about your problems in this manner, you will also find it easier to gain a more rational viewpoint. And if your concerns do not seem to matter anymore, just cut your time of crisis short and enjoy the rest of your day.

Tip 2: Challenge your nervous thoughts

If you are suffering from persistent anxiety and concern, odds are you are looking at the universe in ways that make it sound more dangerous than it is. For example, you could overestimate the likelihood that things could turn out poorly, skip to worst-case scenarios automatically, or treat any nervous thought as though it were a matter of fact. You can even disprove your abilities to deal with life's challenges, assuming you fell apart at the first hint of danger. These modes of thinking, known as cognitive illusions, include:

All-or-nothing philosophy, going at life in the black or white categories, with no middle ground. "If it is not fine, I am a complete loser."

Over-generalization from a single traumatic event, assuming it to be true indefinitely. "I have not been recruited for the role. I am never going to get work."

Focusing on the negatives while filtering the positive. Noting the one thing that went wrong, not just the ones that went right. "I got the last question wrong on the exam. I am such a fool."

Coming up with reasons why good events do not count. "I did well at the presentation, but that was just stupid luck."

Making negative interpretations without any real proof, in other words acting like a mind reader and a fraud at that. For example, "I can tell you she secretly hates me," or, "I just know something horrible is going to happen."

Waiting for the worst-case situation to unfold. "The pilot said that we were in for some turbulence. The plane is going to crash!"

Believing that the way you feel is a reflection of reality. "I feel like I am such an idiot. Someone has to laugh at me."

Have a strict list of what you can and cannot do, and beat yourself up if you break any rules. "I was never supposed to want to initiate a dialogue with her. I am so stupid."

Labeling yourself based on errors and supposed faults. "I am a failure; I am boring; I want to be alone."

Assuming the blame for situations outside your influence. "It is my fault that my son was in an accident. I was supposed to warn him to drive cautiously on the snow."

How to question those thoughts

During your time of worry, question your pessimistic feelings by asking yourself:

- What proof is there that the thought is true?
- Is there a more hopeful, rational way to look at the situation?
- What is the possibility that what I am afraid of would happen? If the likelihood is tiny, what are some of the more probable outcomes?
- Is this thinking helpful? How is it going to support me, and how is it going to hurt me?

Tip 3: Distinguish between solvable and unsolvable problems

Research suggests that when you are worried, you feel less stressed for a while. Running over the issue in your brain distracts you from your feelings and helps you feel like you are getting things done. But there are two very different topics to think about to solve problems.

Problem management includes:

- Assessing the situation.
- Taking specific measures to deal with it.
- Bringing the solution into effect.

Worrying, on the other hand, seldom contributes to a solution. No matter how much time you waste living in worst-case situations, you cannot deal with them if they do happen.

Is your worry resolvable?

Productive, resolvable concerns are those you will take action on right away. For instance, if you are concerned about your payments, you may want to contact your creditors to discuss flexible payment options. Unproductive, unsolvable concerns are those on which there is no corresponding intervention. "What if I get cancer someday?" Or "What if my kid gets into an accident?"

If the worry can be resolved, start brainstorming. Make a list of all the options you might think of. Try not to be too hung up on finding the right answer. Focus on situations that you can change rather than events or realities beyond your grasp. When you have assessed your choices, make an action plan. If you have a strategy and start doing something about the matter, you will be a lot less stressed about it.

If the worry can not be resolvable, embrace the confusion. If you are a pathological worrier, the vast majority of your nervous thoughts are likely to fall into this camp. Worrying is also how we learn to guess what the future holds – a way to avoid unexpected shocks and monitor the results. The thing is that it does not work. Thinking of all the stuff that could go wrong does not make it any more predictable. Focusing on worst-case situations would only distract you from celebrating the positive things you have at present. To stop stressing, address the need for concrete and urgent answers.

Do you like to expect that negative stuff will happen only because they are uncertain? What is the probability that they will?

Given that the risk is very slim, it is easy to survive with a slight probability that something bad might happen.

Ask your friends and family how to deal with confusion in particular circumstances. Will you do the same thing?

Get in touch with your feelings. Worrying over confusion is also a means of avoiding negative emotions. But by tuning in to your thoughts, you can begin to embrace your feelings, including those that are painful or that do not make sense.

Tip 4: Interrupt the loop of concern

It might feel that pessimistic thoughts are racing through your mind in a loop if you overthink. You may think that you are spiraling out of control, going mad, or about to burn out under the weight of all this fear. But there are actions that you can take right now to stop all those nervous feelings and grant yourself a reprieve from anxiety.

Exercise is a safe and successful anti-anxiety therapy that activates endorphins that alleviate pain and stress, increase vitality, and improve your sense of well-being. More specifically, by just reflecting on how your body feels when you walk, you can disrupt the relentless flood of worries that go through your mind. Take in the feeling of your feet touching the ground as you walk, climb, or dance, for example, or the sound of your breath or the feel of sun or wind against your skin.

Take a yoga class or a tai chi workshop. By focusing your attention on your body movements and breathing, performing yoga or tai chi holds your concentration in the moment, helping to clear your mind and contribute to a calm state of mind.

Meditate. Meditation operates by shifting the attention from thinking about the future or living in the past to what is going on right now. You will break the relentless cycle of pessimistic feelings and fears by remaining completely present in the current moment. And there is no need to sit cross-legged, light candles or incense, or chant mantras. Only find a calm, relaxing spot and select one of the many free or affordable mobile applications to help you through the meditation process.

Practice gradual relaxing of muscles. This will help you escape the relentless spiral of worry by concentrating your attention on your body instead of your emotions. By alternately contracting and relaxing various muscle groups in your body, you flex your muscle to relieve some of the tension, and as your body relaxes, your mind is going to comply.

Try to breathe deeply. When you think, you get nervous and breathe harder, sometimes leading to more fear. But by doing deep breathing exercises, you can calm down your mind and quiet stressful thoughts.

Relaxation techniques can change the brain.

While these calming exercises will give some instant respite from worry and fear, doing them daily will also alter the brain. Research has found that daily meditation, for example, will stimulate activation on the left side of the prefrontal cortex, the part of the brain responsible for feelings of serenity and pleasure. The more you train, the more anxiety relief you will receive, and the more control you will begin to have over your nervous thoughts and concerns.

Tip 5: Talk about your concerns

It might sound like a simple answer, but chatting face to face with a trustworthy friend or family member—someone who listens to you without judging, criticizing, or constantly distracting you—is one of the most powerful ways to relax your nervous system and reduce fear. When the concern begins to spiral, talking about them will make them seem even less dangerous.

Keeping you worried encourages the anxieties to build up until they appear unbearable. But speaking about it will help you make sense of what you are doing and put it in context. Whether the concerns are justified or not, verbalizing them will show you what they are. And if your doubts are warranted, sharing them with someone else will give ideas that you would not have thought of on your own. Build a powerful support structure. Human beings are social beings, not capable of living in solitude. But a good support group does not always mean a large network of friends. Do not underestimate the benefits of a few people whom you can rely on to be there for you. And if you do not believe that you have someone to trust, it is never too late to develop new friendships.

Tip 6: Practice conscientiousness

Worrying is normally based on the future—what might happen and what you will do with it—or on the past, rehashing the stuff you have said or done. The centuries-old tradition of mindfulness will help you break away from your fears by turning your attention back to the moment. This approach focuses on observing your concerns and then letting them go, allowing you to recognize where your mindset is causing challenges and getting in contact with your emotions.

Recognize and observe your concerns. Do not ignore, attack, or call them normal. Instead, consider them from an outsider's point of view, without responding or criticizing.

Let go of your fears. Notice that if you are not trying to control the nervous feelings that crop up, they will quickly disappear, like clouds rolling through the sky. It is only when you are engaged in your troubles that you get trapped.

Stay based on the gift. Pay attention to the sounds of your body, to the pattern of your heart, to the ever-changing feelings, and to the thoughts that flow through your head. If you find yourself lost in a single idea, bring your mind back to the current moment.

Repeat every day. Using mindfulness to remain focused on the moment is a straightforward idea, but it requires patience and effort to enjoy its rewards. You will undoubtedly notice at first that your mind keeps going back to your fears. And try not to get upset. Any time you bring your mind back to the moment, you reinforce a new mental pattern that will help you break free from the depressive spiral of anxiety.

Basic therapy on mindfulness

- Find a private spot
- Sit on a comfortable chair or couch, with your back straight, with your palms flat on your upper thighs.
- Close your eyes and breathe in through your nose, allowing the oxygen to flow down through your lower abdomen, in essence breathing into your stomach.
- Breathe out from Your Mouth.
- Focus on the feeling of air rushing into your nose and out of your mouth or your belly rising and dropping as you inhale and exhale.
- If your mind begins to drift, bring it back to breathing with no judgment.
- Try meditation 3 to 4 days a week for 10 minutes a day. Every minute counts.

Chapter 24:
Managing shyness

A shy child is nervous or inhibited when he or she is uncertain or communicates with others. A shy child is more likely to be nervously constrained when they feel they are on display, such as meeting someone unfamiliar or trying to talk in front of others. A shy kid is a lot more relaxed watching the action from the sidelines than jumping in.

Many children feel shy from time to time, but their shyness seriously constrains the lives of others. Children who suffer from intense shyness can grow out of it as they mature or grow up to be shy adults. Parents should help their children overcome moderate shyness.

Complications in timidity

Constant and extreme shyness can reduce the quality of life of a child in many ways, including:

- Reduced opportunities for developing or using social skills
- Fewer colleagues
- Reduced participation in enjoyable and rewarding events involving contact with others, such as sport, dance, drama, or music
- Increased feelings of isolation, lack of value, and lowered self-esteem
- Reduced willingness to achieve maximum capacity due to their fear of being punished

- Embarrassing physical symptoms such as blushing, stammering, and shaking.

Shyness also has optimistic implications.

Shyness is correlated with a variety of constructive behaviors, including:

- Doing well at training.
- Not getting into trouble.
- Listening very attentively to others.
- Being easy to take care of.

Possible sources of timidity

Some of the potential causes of shyness, sometimes in combination, can include:

Genetics: Personality attributes can be determined, at least in part, by the genetic composition of the child.

Personality: Adolescents who are physically sensitive and easily frightened are more likely to grow up to be shy.

Behavioral learning – children learn by imitating their most influential role models: their parents. Shy parents can, by example, 'teach' shyness to their children.

Family relationships – children who may not feel firmly committed to their parents or who have endured poor caregiving may be insecure and vulnerable to shy behavior. Overprotective parents can teach their children to be inhibited and frightened, particularly in unfamiliar circumstances.

Lack of social contact – children, who have been separated from others for the first few years of their life, may not have the social skills to communicate with new people.

Harsh criticism – children who are mocked or harassed by important people in their lives (parents, peers, and other close family members or friends) may appear to be shy.

Fear of failure – children that have been forced so many times beyond their capacities (and then made to feel guilty because they have not 'measured up') may have perceptions of failure that manifest as shyness.

The Human nature

If children are behaving shy in a social setting, they could bet on their actions afterward. This self-reproach will make them more self-aware and increase the risk of a child acting shyly in the future. As time goes by, their confidence and self-esteem will begin to diminish. The less secure the infant is, the more likely they are to act in a shy manner.

Parental behaviors are of critical significance. Suggested suggestions include:

- Be sure not to mark your child as 'shy.' Children (and adults) prefer to live up to the names that others assign them.
- Do not let anyone mark your child as timid, either.
- Never judge or ridicule your kid when they are shy. Be supportive, empathetic, and understanding.
- Encourage your child to chat about the reasons behind their timidity and ask what they are scared of?

- Tell your child at all times of your life that you were shy and how you conquered it. Since young children frequently see their parents as ideal, admitting to your timidity will help your child feel better and lessen their overall timidity.
- Just be outgoing yourself. Model confident conduct and lead by example.

Professional assistance

If your child's shyness is particularly crippling, you might want to seek clinical advice from a counselor or a psychologist. Treatment choices include:

- Regulation of stress.
- Relaxation policy.
- Sessions and counseling.
- Training in social skills.

Chapter 25:
Overcoming perfectionism

Perfectionism is a robber.

Perfectionism—refusing to stand for something short of perfection—steals from you all the following:

It steals your pleasure.

It robs you of your self-confidence.

It steals the desire to do stuff.

It takes away your passion.

It robs you of your self-acceptance.

It robs you of your opportunity to grow.

If you have perfectionist inclinations, as many people do, use the following tips below to conquer it:

1. Accept that you are a perfectionist. Some people do not even know that they are perfectionists. They may be convincing themselves that they only have high aspirations and aim for perfection. However, there is a distinction between quality and perfectionism. The following questions will allow you to find out whether you are a perfectionist:

Are you having trouble meeting your standards?

Do you have crippling fears of failure?

Do you think the faults are landmines (instead of stepping stones)?

Do people always say you have unreasonable expectations?

Is your self-confidence based on your achievements?

If you replied "yes" to all of the above questions, you have a problem with perfectionism.

2. Recognize the difference between healthy drive and perfectionism. Wanting to change yourself—whether you are gaining weight, increasing the pace of running, reading more books, getting better at public speaking, and so on—is positive. There is, however, a distinction between balanced striving and perfectionism.

Brené Brown, an American academic, blogger, and public speaker, defines healthy aspiration as achieving achievement from a position of dignity.

Perfectionism, on the other hand, stems from a belief that it is not good enough. Perfectionists believe that once they meet a particular standard, they will eventually feel good about themselves.

To put it differently, healthy striving is about honoring yourself and striving to reach your full potential. Perfectionism is about dishonoring yourself and convincing yourself that there are certain things you need to do before you are "enough."

3. Set practical goals. Perfectionists have set targets that are entirely out of their reach. Then they spend a few months feeling furious and depressed because no matter what their target is, they are still a long way off from achieving it. The answer is to start setting practical expectations.

When you hit your achievable target, set another goal that's only a little further down. Keep up this pace this way, and you will quickly find that you have made many strides.

4. Define 'Must-Haves' and 'Nice-to-Haves.' Suppose you are a house hunter. The first thing you ought to do is to define your "must-have" features. These may be anything like the following:

- Three bedrooms, two bathrooms.
- A large kitchen.
- Quiet neighborhood.
- Nice school district.
- Lots of sunlight.

Then think about your "nice-to-have" features. This may include the following:

- A fireplace.
- A swimming pool.
- A den.
- A patio

Now you have got two options. You can either look for a house that contains only your "must-have" features, or you can search for a house that includes both your "must-have" and "nice-to-have" features.

Of course, a house that includes all kinds of amenities will take longer to locate and cost more. So the question is: can you afford the extra cost—in terms of both time and money—for the "nice-to-have" features?

For whatever you do, you can ask yourself the same questions:

What are the "must-have" characteristics of this?

What are the "nice-to-have" features?

While perfectionists seem to try to have "nice-to-have" features in everything they do, in most instances, "must-have" features are good enough.

Have the "nice-to-have" functionality only if the added work is worth it, and you have the time and money to do so.

5. To lower the expectations. A major challenge for perfectionists is setting expectations that are far too high. You can correct this by dropping the expectations. Instead of shooting for what you believe to be 100 %, target for what seems like a 90 % commitment on your part. Then, examine what happened:

Is the sky been falling?

Is the manager mad that the job was not good enough?

Has anyone complained?

Was the customer frustrated?

Were there any negative implications?

If all was well with your 90% commitment, consider dropping your expectations to 80%. Is it all right? Then consider even lowering the expectations.

Of course, the goal here is not to start doing stuff on a subpar level but to test the expectations to make them more practical.

6. Try some new stuff. Perfectionists have a deep fear of committing mistakes. And all this does is to hold them back. After all, making errors is how we grow. Besides, being able to accept errors is a critical aspect of creativity and risk-taking.

One way to conquer the fear of making mistakes is to do new stuff. By encouraging yourself to make mistakes in places where you are a complete newbie, will make you feel more relaxed making mistakes in other areas of your life.

7. Step away from things that deepen your perfectionist tendencies. A while back, I watched a TV show where the star was this beautiful lady who was a genius neurosurgeon. She attended the best academic institutions in the United States and speaks many languages. When they said she was also a marathon runner, I changed the channel.

The culture around us imposes impossibly high standards: corporate gurus tell us to produce too soon constantly.

You hear slogans like this all the time: "No one remembers who takes second place."

Any magazine you open is packed with impeccable body models.

Everyone on Facebook fabricates having a perfect marriage, a perfect child, a perfect home, a perfect company.

It just does not stop there. Move away from all the things that affirm your tendency to perfection:

Avoid reading magazines that make you feel like you are going to crash.

Remove someone on Twitter who goes on all the time about how perfect their lives are.

Avoid people who make you feel like whatever you do is not good enough.

Do this instead:

- Read stuff that empowers you.
- Join with people who support you as you are and inspire you to be even better off.
- Join people on social media who encourage and empower you.

8. Accept that you will never be done. The other day, I read an article written by a woman with twin boys. She complained that she always had stuff on her plate.

If one twin was crying and finally tried to get him to sleep, the other twin would wake up a minute later and start crying. As soon as she changed the diaper of one twin, the other twin had to be changed.

That is exactly what it is like. Consider the following:

You may have attained your perfect weight and are doing very well at work, but then your significant other loses his job, and your relationship starts to crumble because of the tension that this creates.

Then you get it back on track, but your boss is leaving, and it is not easy to replace her.

You spend many months applying for a new job, and you find one that's much better than the job you have been doing. However, when you were busy working on getting a foothold in the new company, you did not have time to work out, so you added weight.

Do you see the cycle? Existence is like running on a treadmill. And if you were to get to the point that almost everything about your life is "perfect"—and this is a major "if"—it is almost sure to be short-lived. To conquer perfectionism, accept that you will never be "done."

9. Enjoy the ride. Perfectionists fix their attention on the destination. That is all that matters to them. In reality, they are so focused on the destination that they cannot enjoy the trip.

Bear in mind that the destination is the cherry on top in order to conquer the perfectionist tendencies. The voyage is the ice cream, the fudge, the cream, the caramel, and the cream of the marshmallow. Look at the following:

- You cannot run a 10 kilometers marathon yet, but feel satisfied that you can run 6 kilometers today.
- You cannot quit your day's work yet, but be proud that your side business is growing day by day
- You really cannot perform Beethoven's Moonlight Sonata on the piano, but you can play the pieces you know with pleasure.

Chapter 26:
How To Help Children Who Have Anxiety About The Doctor & Shots

Let us be honest: few of us look forward to visits to the doctor, but when kids are afraid to go to the doctor, parents know that even run-of-the-mill tests will turn into big meltdowns. I have come up with some ideas to help your family get a smoother next visit.

Be clear about what will happen

For children who are afraid to go to the hospital, learning what to expect will greatly help them. "Because children are afraid to go to the hospital, they sometimes envision something even worse than what is going to happen," says Dr. Rachel Busman, a pediatric psychologist at the Child Mind Institute. "They might fear that something is going to hurt, or they might believe that needing to see a doctor means they are sick."

Likewise, Dr. Busman suggests that children who do not expect a shot—or a long wait—and get one are more likely to get nervous or irritated than people who know beforehand. Determining how the appointment is going step-by-step will help your child control his or her hopes and anxieties.

Avoid using blanket words or ambiguous explanations such as: "The doctor is going check you up." Instead, describe each step in a simple, thorough manner that your child will readily understand: "After we go to the exam room, the doctor will check your pulse using an instrument called a stethoscope..."

Do not over-promise

When your kid asks the BIG question—"Am I going to get a shot?"—it may be enticing to convince him that, even if you are not 100% positive, he will not require one. So it is best to be frank about what you know—and what you do not know.

"It is not necessary to lie," says Dr. Bernhard Wiedermann, an infectious disease physician at the Children's National Health System in Washington, D.C. "It is easier to suggest, 'I am not sure, so we should ask the doctor when we get there.'" Being easy will help create trust and guarantee that your child does not feel deceived or blindsided if things do not go as expected.

Validate sentiments

"When children are nervous, as parents we want to tell them, 'It will be all right! There is nothing to be scared of," says Dr. Busman. "But we are shutting the kid down by doing so." Instead, she suggests, parents affirm emotions and model healthier ways to cope with fear by offering themselves as Exhibit A.

"I understand how you feel," for example. "Before my doctor's appointment last week, I was very anxious, but I am glad I went. It is how we remain safe and healthy."

Work with concerns of your child

Once you have thought about how the doctor's appointment will go, give your kid a chance to talk to you about why he is nervous and ask if he has any questions. "The kids do not know how to describe what they are feeling," says Dr. Busman. "If your child says, 'I do not want to go. I am afraid,'" he said, "help him think on the particulars of what he feels worried about. That is how you can handle it more efficiently."

If your kid has a hard time voicing his or her thoughts, consider posing questions to help him narrow it down. For example, "Let us go over all that's going to happen tomorrow. Stop me before we get to something that sounds terrifying, so we can think of ways to make things less frightening before we leave."

Manage your anxiety first

When your child does not feel well, he will not be the only one to feel nervous. When kids are sick, it is easy to be anxious, but it is vital to handle their anxiety correctly.

"If you feel nervous or have questions that may not be prudent to pose in front of your child, ask to speak to the doctor while your child is being examined," says Dr. Wiedermann. "It will help your child keep happy and allow you a chance to let the doctor know your questions before the consultation starts."

Support the doctor

"As doctors, we intend our patients and their families to feel secure," says Dr. Wiedermann, "and getting feedback from their parents can be very useful."

Examples of helpful feedback may be:

Ask the doctor to calm down and explain it step by step.

Ask her to use child-friendly words so that your child will be part of the conversation.

"Many physicians who deal with children have tricks to make children feel more comfortable, but not all of them work with all children," says Dr. Pamela Parker, a pediatrician in Silver Spring, Maryland. It is also essential for parents to let the doctor know what worked for their child and what did not.

It is of great benefit for some kids to be part of the process, while others do not find it helpful. "It is not obvious straight away how kids feel in the exam room," says Dr. Parker, "but it is good for us if parents give feedback, 'He liked being your helper last time. Will you do that again?' Or, 'You know, I do not think he liked to wear a stethoscope, could we do something new this time?'"

Bring distractions

Your child will be seen on time every time in an ideal universe, but you are more likely to waste at least a little time in your doctor's waiting room. Many pediatricians have toys, but if your child is nervous, do not depend on an old copy of Highlights magazine to help him remain calm. Instead, let him pick a favorite game or book to bring along that will help keep his mind busy as he waits.

The straight talk of shots

"The child will have to get a shot at some point," says Dr. Busman, "so it is necessary to psyche them about it." A good dose of honesty—and perspective—is the only way forward when it comes to shots.

Be simple: "No one wants to have injections, but they are a huge part of what keeps us safe, so sometimes we just have to get them."

Make it quick: if the idea of having a shot towards the end of the procedure leads to your child's fear, consider coordinating with the doctor ahead of time to see if it is possible to have it out of the way at the beginning of the visit. Don't put it off: "Kids do all manner of stuff to put the shots off," says Dr. Parker, but she says it is best not to give in. "If your kid does not get a shot now, he is going to need one next time."

Put it in perspective: For most children (and some adults), the terror of getting a shot is generally even greater than the shot itself. "Learn to put things in context," says Dr. Busman. "Remember the last time you had a shot? It was done fast, and then you went to basketball practice!"

Get it over with: "Needle phobia is a real thing," says Dr. Parker, "and for some kids, being rational is not a choice in the moment." In those situations, she said the only thing parents should do is help the kid stay as calm as possible and wait for the storm to pass. "When the shot is done, the kids who were shouting bloody murder just a moment earlier would think, 'Wow, is that all?'" says Dr. Parker. "The trick is to get it done as soon as possible and then carry on."

When the shots are done, give gratitude and a compliment: "I am so proud of you. You were afraid, but you did it anyway! That was courageous."

When it is more than just a little fear

Many of the kids are a little afraid of going to the hospital, so once the Band-Aid is on and they are out the door, they go on to the next thing. Persistent or serious anxiety may be a symptom of something more severe. Signals to watch for include:

- Your child starts to wonder about a doctor's appointment weeks or even months before a check-up is planned.

- Your child also shows the fear that they, or another family member, will be severely sick or die.
- He is obsessed with the appointment of a doctor or his health even after the visit has finished.
- Anxiety over seeing a doctor inhibits his capacity to concentrate on other activities.

It's time to consult a professional for help.

Chapter 27:
How to help your child managing Stress

Children can seem carefree to adults. However, the kids also experience tension. Stuff like education and their social life can be reasons for children feeling stressed. As a parent, you can't shield your children from stress—but you can help them learn healthier ways to deal with stress and overcome daily problems.

Kids deal with tension in both safe and unhealthy ways. And while they might not start a dialogue about what bothers them, they want their parents to reach out to help them deal with their problems.

But it's not always straightforward for parents to decide what to do for a kid who feels overwhelmed.

Here are a couple of ideas:

Let them know you know something isn't right. Tell your child that something is bothering him or her. If you can, mention the emotion that you believe your child is experiencing. ('It appears you're still angry about what happened at the playground.') This isn't supposed to feel like an indictment (as in, "Okay, well, what has happened now? Are you angry at that? ") or to put a kid on the spot. It should sound like you're just interested in hearing about your child's concerns. Be respectful and prove you care and want to learn.

Listen to your kids. Let your child tell you what is wrong. Listen attentively and calmly—with curiosity, tolerance, openness, and care. Avoid the desire to criticize, accuse, teach, or suggest what you believe your child should do instead. The idea is to consider the needs (and feelings) of your child. Try to get the entire story by posing questions like "And so what happened?" Take the time. And let the child take his time, too.

Comment quickly on the emotions you believe your child has been having. For example, you might say, "you must have been angry," "No wonder you felt crazy when you weren't allowed to play," or "That must have seemed unreasonable to you." This shows you know what your child felt and why he felt that way and that you care about. Feeling heard and listened to makes your child feel embraced by you, and this is particularly crucial in times of stress.

Put a name on it. Many younger children don't have words for their emotions yet. When your child is irritated or upset, use these terms to help them learn to recognize feelings by name. Putting emotions into writing helps children connect and gain emotional awareness—the capacity to understand their emotional states. Children who can do so are less likely to hit a behavioral tipping point where intense feelings emerge through actions rather than words.

Help your child learn about things to do. When there is a real situation that causes discomfort, speak to each other about what to do. Encourage your child to learn a few ideas. If required, you should start brainstorming, but don't do all the work. Active engagement by your child will create morale. Support and add to the positive ideas as needed. Ask, "How do you think this is going to work?"

Listen to the child and move on— Often, speaking and listening, and feeling heard is all that is required to make a child's frustrations begin to melt away. After that, strive to change the focus and move on to something more constructive and calming. Help your child think of what to do to make himself feel better. Don't pay more attention to the issue than it merits.

Limit tension where possible. If there are circumstances that trigger anxiety, see if there are options to change anything. For example, if too many after-school activities regularly make it impossible to complete homework, it could be necessary to restrict activities to leave time and energy for homework.

Just be right there. Let your kids know that you're going to be there any time they feel like communicating. When kids don't want to speak to, they normally don't want parents to leave them alone. You will make your child happier by just being there—keeping him or her company, sharing time. So if you find that your child appears to be in the dumps, depressed, or has had a rough day—but doesn't feel like talking—start something you can do together: take a stroll, watch a movie, shoot some hoops, or bake some cookies. Isn't it good to know that your presence counts?

Be polite. It hurts to see your child upset or stressed as a mom. But continue to fight the temptation to solve all problems. Instead, concentrate on having your child, slowly but gradually, develop into a strong problem-solver—a kid who knows how to roll up and down with life, put emotions into words, settle down when needed, and bounce up to try again.

Parents can't fix all dilemmas as children go about their lives. But by teaching safe coping skills, you're training your kids to handle future problems.

Finding opportunities to get the tension out of their minds can make children feel happier about themselves. For each person, the best ways to alleviate stress are different. Test some of these suggestions to see which ones work for your child:

Exercise- A daily routine is one of the easiest ways to cope with tension. For youngsters, this includes walking, biking, outdoor play, and individual and group sports.

Write it or draw it- Older children also find it useful to write about problems that concern them. Younger children can draw theirs.

Let your emotions out— Invite your child to speak, laugh, scream, and show anger when they need to.

Participate in fun activities- A hobby could help your child relax. Volunteer service or work that benefits people may be a big stress relief for older children.

Learn how to relax- This can include breathing exercises, muscle-calming exercises, massage, aromatherapy, meditation, prayer, yoga, or soothing exercises such as tai chi and qi gong.

Chapter 28:
How to help your child Make Friends

How do we help children make friends? It may appear that we can do very little. Making friends is, after all, a very personal business.

But building friendship relies on the child's emotional abilities, self-regulation skills, and social maturity. Parents play an important role in the growth of these skills.

For example, a lot of kids have difficulty making friends because they feel nervous or insecure. If children are taught how to react to friendly openings—and provide them with simple, secure opportunities to engage with friendly people—it will help them develop important social connections.

Likewise, some adolescents suffer when they lack proper self-control or respond in antagonistic ways to others. These kids will find it much easier to make friends if we help them improve their self-regulation skills.

And nearly every child would benefit from coaching and training in the social arts. Effective friendships around the world rely on the same core skills. To be effective, children must regulate their own negative emotions. They must:

- understand other people's feelings and perspectives;
- show sympathy and help those in need;
- feel confident and confident towards others;

- know how to handle introductions and engage in conversation;
- be able to cooperate, negotiate and compromise;
- know how to apologize and make amends,
- be understanding.

It's a long list, and it takes experience, commitment, and practice to hone these skills.

So that's why parents and teachers should be supportive. There is no magic trick to making friends. It's something we learn to do.

So here is an evidence-based guide—12 tangible ways we can help children make friends.

1. Show warmth and reverence to your kids. Don't attempt to manipulate your kid by threatening, punishing, or blackmailing emotionally.

It does not seem to be of direct significance to your child's desire to make friends. But the way parents treat children affects their mental maturity and social behavior. And this will affect their peer relationships.

For example, strict parenting, a caregiving style that stresses total discipline, low levels of warmth, and an effort to regulate actions by threatening, punishing, or mocking.

In studies undertaken worldwide, strict parenting has been attributed to the emergence of behavioral disorders (Lansford et al., 2018). And kids with behavioral issues have more difficulty finding friends.

Parental psychological control—the effort to exploit children by guilt trips, bullying, or withholding affection—makes children grow poor-quality friendships (e.g., Cook et al., 2012).

On the other hand, as parents show affection and use constructive discipline techniques – reasoning with children and explaining the rules – children appear to become more pro-social over time.

They're most inclined to treat people with empathy and compassion (Pastorelli et al., 2015).

They seem to be less aggressive, more self-reliant, and more like peers.

2. Be an "emotional mentor" for your kids.

We all feel depressive thoughts and selfish desires. Can that keep us from keeping healthy friendships? Well, the answer is No unless we know how to keep these feelings under control.

So children need to learn how to handle their feelings. And what can we do as parents? We can support them, or we can make it worse.

For example, in one study, researchers asked parents— mothers to five-year-olds—how they reacted to their children's negative emotions. The researchers then monitored children's results over many years.

Kids were more likely to acquire good self-regulation abilities if they grew up with an adult who spoke to them – sympathetically and constructively – on how to deal with bad moods and unpleasant emotions (Blair et al., 2013). And the better the child's self-regulation abilities, the more likely the child was to develop healthy peer interactions as they grew older.

On the other hand, reports show that children acquire poor self-regulation abilities when their parents respond dismissively ("You're just stupid!") or punitively ("Go to your room!") to their children's negative emotions.

So when children get angry, it's worth taking the time to consider their emotions and consciously teach them how to treat these feelings in a positive, meaningful manner.

3. Encourage the child's capacity to empathize and "read the mind."

Children need to do more than regulate their negative feelings. They need to consider other people's emotions and viewpoints.

"Isn't this stuff going to come naturally?" one may ask. Maybe, however, "naturally" does not mean "automatically— without motivation and assistance." There are tangible steps that parents and teachers should take to help children develop their feelings.

4. Is your kid socially anxious? Have a safe social atmosphere.

It's hard for children to make friends if they feel very nervous about it. So what can we do about it?

Sensitive, attentive parenting is particularly critical for socially insecure children. They deserve to know that we're going to be there for them anytime they need us. As I mentioned earlier, research shows that sensitive, attentive parenting helps children establish a stable relationship that promotes trust and freedom.

But when children truly deal with fear, they need extra help.

They see the environment as particularly threatening. If we don't resolve it, they are likely to have chronic relational problems—problems that can interfere with the growth of social skills and make it very difficult for a kid to make friends.

So if your kid has a high level of anxiety, speak to your pediatrician or school psychologist. Child professionals have also created proven therapies for psychiatric distress through cognitive behavioral counseling, an approach intended to re-train a child's misconceptions and overreactive emotional reactions (Seligman and Ollendick 2011).

But it is still essential to bear in mind: often, the risks are genuine.

For example, your child could be attending a school where violent behavioral issues are normal. Your child may be conscious of peers or neighbors who have suffered abuse. Or maybe he is being subjected to threats, peer dismissal, or abuse.

If this is the situation with your kid, it makes sense to do what you can to change your child's life. This requires steps to deter abuse, intimidation, and harassment. But it can also include finding your child a new social outlet—like a club or a playgroup—that is particularly accommodating and safe.

5. Address the violent or destructive behavioral issues of your infant.

As I discussed above, such behavioral issues can pose a significant social barrier to making friends.

6. Teach your child important conversation skills.

To make new friends, children need to learn how to relate with others and think about the right words to say.

They should learn how to listen to each other, and they need to know how to give conversational feedback—to prove that they understand what was being said.

How are we going to foster these skills?

We will help by demonstrating positive listening habits at home and involving our children in fun, reciprocal conversations (Feldman et al., 2013).

Besides, we will benefit by consciously educating children on what to do and what to say.

For example, children profit when we teach them the art of "active listening."

This is where a person makes it apparent that he or she is paying attention—by making proper eye contact, orienting the body in the speaker's direction, staying still, and making significant verbal responses.

Psychologists Fred Frankel and Robert Myatt agree on the fact that we should train children to become stronger conversationalists by giving them these concrete tips:

When you start a conversation with someone new, exchange your "likes" and "dislikes."

Don't be an interviewer. Don't just ask your questions—offer details about yourself.

Don't be a puppy in conversation. If you are engaging in a dialogue, provide answers to asked questions. Give your companion a chance to speak when you're done.

If you need more chances for your child to practice? Please try a phone call or an online video chat.

7. Host social events that promote cooperation—not rivalry.

Studies show that children get better off as they partake in group activities—activities in which children collaborate for a shared purpose (Roseth et al. 2008). This is true in the classroom, and it is also true when children play (Gelb and Jacobson 1988).

So if children struggle socially, it's usually a smart idea to keep them away from competitive sports, at least before they learn proper social skills (Frankel and Myatt 2002).

Fred Frankel and Robert Myatt propose the following additional advice: If your child has a play date, don't include toys and games that could cause a confrontation. They suggest, for example, that parents exclude toy guns, as well as other things that may cause rivalry or jealousy. If your kid has a precious something that he or she can't afford to reveal, it's best to put it away till the date is over.

8. Show the child how to deal with difficult social conditions.

Suppose a girl, Sophie, sees a few children playing together. Sophie wishes to visit them, but she doesn't know how to do so. What is she supposed to do?

Victoria Finnie and Alan Russell (Finnie and Russell 1988) posed this hypothetical case to the mothers of preschool girls, asking them to weigh in. Interestingly, the mothers who had the right recommendations were often the mothers whose children had the best social skills.

What did the wise mothers say?

Before you go over, watch what the other kids are doing. What would you do to blend in with that?

Try to enter the game by doing something important. For example, if kids are playing a restaurant game, see if you can become a new customer.

Don't be noisy or critical, or try to change the game.

If the other children don't want you to participate, don't try to push them. Only get back out of there and find something else to do.

It's helpful advice that we should pass on to our children. Children thrive as we help them come up with distinct ways to cope with difficult social problems.

9. Help children understand the art of consensus and negotiation.

To develop healthy relationships with peers, children need to learn peaceful ways of resolving disputes. They need to consider what other people need and want; they need to anticipate the effects of different actions.

Kids who grow up with brothers and sisters have an integrated benefit in learning these abilities. They have a lot of opportunities to learn the art of negotiation.

Although you don't have to have siblings to develop strong social skills, all children—regardless of their family composition—can learn given a little guidance and training. Studies show that children can improve their skills by role-playing games and programs that challenge them to answer potential social conflicts.

The next time your child has a disagreement with someone else, make it a learning experience. Help your child think about a compromise that is fair to both sides.

10. Show the child how to express regret and make amendments.

Everyone makes a mess of things at one point or the other. We make poor decisions and causing harm or hurt the feelings of others.

What happens next? If we feel ashamed or "canceled" because of our failures, we prefer to dwell on our negative feelings. We feel shame, frustration, even rage, and it doesn't allow us to rebuild our social connections- far from it.

On the other hand, imagine what happens if we have a feeling of remorse. Feeling guilty can be positive. We focus on how our behaviors have influenced others. We have solidarity for our victims. And it encourages us to try to undo the harm that we have done.

This distinction is key to making and retaining friends.

Studies confirm that children—even children as young as four years of age—are more likely to forgive a peer for misconduct if that peer actively apologizes. And as children grow older (and become more sophisticated), they pay attention to whether the perpetrator's signals are remorseful. They do not always need an overt apology—not if they notice signs of guilt (Oostenbroek and Vaish 2019).

So what is the most successful way to fix a relationship? Don't just apologize or show regret. Make amends.

In a 6-and 7-year-old clinical trial, researchers studied how children reacted to a transgressor who knocked down a tower they were constructing. Kids forgave when the transgressor apologized, but they felt angry. The only thing that made these children feel better was if the transgressor deliberately helped them restore their tower (Drell and Jaswal 2015).

So that's what we should try to do—to show our children how to fix relationships. From a very early age, we should train them on how to apologize and make amends for their mistakes.

11. Encourage your child to recognize and forgive other people's mistakes.

Kids may be forgiving, but it doesn't necessarily come easily. In reality, certain children have a persistent problem with vindictiveness. They prefer to believe that other people are hostile, and they can be indignant over alleged slights and insults.

If that's your child's dilemma, you're going to want to help change his or her views of others. Have your child understand the transgressor's perspective and ask your child to consider possible reasons for problematic conduct.

It could have been an honest mistake. Perhaps the transgressor was stressing out over something or feeling exhausted or sick. Maybe the transgressor just had a bad day, and you happened to get in his way.

When adults ask children to consider possible theories, children are more likely to give the offenders the benefit of the doubt.

Of course, not every action deserves prodding. Many children are too indulgent towards wrongdoers. They blame themselves as they become abused and stay in relationships that leave them perpetually exploited or mistreated (Luchies et al. 2010).

So we need to be conscious of the circumstances and give each child the kind of care they deserve.

12. Observe your child's social life, but be vigilant about being too controlling—especially as your child gets older.

Studies in several cultures show that children are better off when their parents remain aware of their social interactions (Parke et al. 2002).

Parental control involves monitoring where young children play, helping children find ways to interact and socialize with fun, pro-social peers, chatting to classmates of your children as they come to visit, and telling your children to tell you about the stuff they do in their spare time.

There is also research supporting setting such boundaries, such as demanding that your teenager tell you in advance about the specifics of an evening outing.

"Whom are you going to hang out with? What are you going to do? Where are you going?" Parents can embarrass their children—and scare off future friends—by being too invasive.

And if the kids see us being too controlling, they're more likely to ignore our advice. In fact, in one study, teenagers were more likely to pick a delinquent peer as a friend if they felt their parents overexerted their control (Tilton-Weaver et al., 2013).

It is also necessary to give your child a sense of autonomy and to express your questions in a manner that appears rational and respectful. Otherwise, your child will come to see your authority as unconstitutional and act as he or she likes.

Chapter 29:
Help your child not to be afraid of school

School prevention – also known as refusal to attend school or school phobia – is not unusual and happens in as many as 5% of children. These children may refuse to attend kindergarten, or they may give excuses why they do not go.

They may miss a lot of learning by claiming to have confusing, inexplicable ailments. Many of these children have signs of anxiety, over which they have no conscious control. They may have headaches, stomach aches, hyperventilation, nausea, or dizziness

The signs of a child shirking school typically manifest on school days and are usually absent on weekends. When a doctor treats these children, no real diseases are found or diagnosed.

School-Related Anxiety:

Often, children who avoid school do not know exactly why they feel sick, and they may have trouble expressing what causes their pain or discomfort.

School-related fear causes children to refuse to attend school. Some of these fears include:

- Afraid of separation from parents or caregiver
- Problems with other kids (for instance, teasing because they are "fat" or "short."

- Anxieties around toileting in a public bathroom
- Threats to physical harm (as from a school bully)
- Actual bodily harm

Advice for concerned parents:

As a first move, school-avoidance management entails visiting a psychiatrist who may rule out physical illness and support parents in developing a recovery plan. Once a medical disorder has been dismissed as a source of the child's symptoms, parents' actions should be focused not only on considering the stresses that the child is undergoing but also on getting them back to school.

Here are only some recommendations to help your child solve this problem:

Speak to your kid on whether he or she doesn't want to go to kindergarten. Consider and state all the possibilities. Be sympathetic, helpful, and consider why he or she is angry. Work to overcome the unpleasant circumstances that the two of you perceive as being the source of the problem.

Recognize that you appreciate your child's needs, but focus on his or her prompt return to education. The more your child remains at home, the more complicated his or her inevitable return would be. Clarify that they are in good health and that their problems are likely due to worries about other factors, like grades, homework, teacher relationships, anxieties about peer pressure, or genuine concern about school abuse. Let your child know that school attendance is expected by statute. He or she will try to use any leverage they on you to stay at home, but you must be committed to getting your child back to school.

Talk about your child avoiding school with the school staff, including their coach, the principal, and the school nurse. Share the preparations for your child's return to school with them and enlist their help and assistance.

Be extra-firm on school nights, when children frequently worry about their symptoms. Keep debates on anxieties to a minimum. For example, don't ask your child how he or she feels, whether he or she is well enough to be up and about the home, either he or she is well enough to attend kindergarten.

Your child's pediatrician may help ease your child's adjustment back into school by writing a note verifying that he or she has symptoms that prevented the child from attending school, so while the symptoms may continue, he or she is now able to go back to school.

Ask the school staff for assistance with your child when he or she is in school. A school nurse or secretary will take care of your child if they become symptomatic and encourage them to return to the classroom.

If a situation such as a school bully or an unreasonable teacher is the source of your child's distress, become the child's advocate and address these topics with school staff. The teacher or principal might need to make some changes to ease the burden on your kid in the classroom or the playground.

If your child stays at home on a school day, make sure they are safe and happy but do not give any special care. Whether your child's complaint warrants it, he or she should lie in bed. There should be no special snacks, no guests, and he or she should be watched carefully.

Your child may perhaps need to see a doctor while he or she is at home due to a physical illness. Reasons to stay at home can include fatigue, fever higher than 101 degrees, vomiting, diarrhea, rash, cough, earache, or toothache.

Help your child gain independence by promoting activities with other children outside the house. This can include sporting events and evenings with friends.

Chapter 30:
How to Help your Child During Panic Attacks

Panic attacks are abrupt and unforeseen bouts of extreme anxiety, which may have no apparent causes and may occur when the individual least expects. Panic attacks can be particularly terrifying, and this is particularly so if a child is the victim.

It can be painful to observe your child battle panic attacks. You may feel powerless, and you may not know what to do differently, so it doesn't happen. However, it's vital to remember that you're not alone and that there are steps you can take to support your child.

What are the signs of panic attacks?

Panic attacks can lead to various psychological and physical effects that can differ from person to person. Your child may feel as if he or she has lost control and is stuck or unable to free himself or herself from certain circumstances. Panic episodes can also be preceded by physical effects, which may include:

- Feeling weak, dizzy, or light-headed.
- Feeling nauseous
- Abdominal discomfort;
- Chest pressure and shortness of breath
- Palpitations of the heart
- Fluctuating body temperature
- Hyperventilation

In most situations, panic attacks last for a few minutes before they subside. However, signs can also make patients think that they have a heart attack, making them worry about another panic attack, leading to a vicious spiral.

What triggers child panic attacks?

Like other mental health disorders, evidence shows that there could be various causes that may raise the risk that your child may have a panic attack. This includes the following:

- Hereditary/genetic causes – study suggests that having a close partner (such as a parent or a sibling) who has panic disorders makes it more likely that a child may also have panic attacks.
- Phobias-Children can suffer panic attacks as a result of being exposed to something they fear.
- Present mental health conditions such as fear, depression, obsessive-compulsive disorder (OCD), or post-traumatic stress disorder (PTSD)
- Short-term mental stimuli such as bereavement
- Low self-esteem;
- Certain stimulants can also cause signs of a panic attack in infants, including caffeine.

Steps that you should take to help your child deal with panic attacks

There are various things you can do as a parent to help your child deal with panic attacks.

- Stay in control of yourself during a panic attack.

When your kid has a panic attack, they're likely to feel like they've lost control. That's why it's so crucial that you remain in control. Try to stay calm and speak to them in a soft, soothing voice. Tell them to take deep breaths and reassure them that the attack will soon be over. Once the panic attack appears to have subsided, allow them plenty of time and room to cool down.

- Breathing exercise

Explain to your child that their breathing gets heavier when during a panic attack, making them feel light-headed, dizzy, and cause chest pain. Teach them to slow down their breathing; this will help alleviate the physical effects of a panic attack and allow the panic attack to pass quicker. Tell your child to breathe through their nose for three seconds, hold their breath for two seconds, and then exhale fully. Your kid will be able to follow this breathing technique the next time they have a panic attack.

- Teach your kid about Panic Attacks

Panic attacks can be terrifying, and the child may be worried about a whole host of things, ranging from worrying about people laugh at them to worrying that they're getting a heart attack or even dying. By educating your child about panic attacks, you can help dispel some of these fears. Tell your child that panic attacks are normal and not dangerous, even if attacks feel frightening and life-threatening. Reassure them that the panic episodes are short and will shortly come to an end.

- Encourage your kid to face their fears

If your child has panic attacks in reaction to certain circumstances or objects, it is necessary to allow them to confront their fears. For instance, if your child becomes panicked while he or she is in the vehicle, gradually introduce them to vehicles in carefully graded stages, such as staying in the car when they are parked, before stepping progressively up to ride in the car on very brief journeys. This will make your child appreciate that their fears are unfounded. Give your child a lot of praise and motivation during this time, and assure them that they don't have to fight alone.

- Challenge the negative thoughts

The way your child feels about problems will affect their level of fear. Many of their emotions may be out of their control. Therefore, it's important to make your child understand that these are just feelings, not reality. If your child believes many of their unhelpful thoughts during a panic attack, these thoughts should be questioned since they are often based on false assumptions.

- Help your child change their focus.

Your kid is likely to experience a lot of pessimistic feelings during a panic attack. You can help to shift their attention from these feelings by allowing them to focus on something important, preferably something that soothes or comforts them. It could be a favorite doll, a picture of something nice, or a pet. You may even help your child create a 'happy spot' within their brain they can escape to. Encourage them to remember a situation or a scenario where they feel relaxed and secure, and tell them to reflect on it if they feel panicked.

- Reassure your child that there are people to lean on for support.

It's essential to let your child know that they never have to suffer on their own; someone will always be there to support and listen to them. Tell your child's teachers about their panic attacks, and encourage them to step in if your child gets one in school. Encourage your child to talk to someone and be near someone if they suspect a panic attack is coming on.

- Get help

While these measures will help you comfort your child, they will need clinical assistance if they have frequent panic attacks.

NOTES

PART 4

RAISING WITH SELF LOVE

Chapter 31:
Raise Yourself before you Raise your Child

Self-esteem is your child's passport to a future of mental wellbeing and social happiness. It is the cornerstone of a child's wellbeing and the secret to great achievements as an adult. How you feel about yourself determines how you behave at all times. Try some tips and advice to better raise a child with high self-esteem.

Self-image is how one sees oneself.

A boy looks in the mirror, and he likes the guy he sees. He looks inside himself, and he's happy with the guy he sees. He must think of himself as someone who can make things happen and who is deserving of love. Parents are the principal cause of a child's self-esteem.

Lack of good self-image leads to behavioral problems.

Many of the behavioral issues I see in therapy stem from both parent's and children's low self-esteem. Why is one human a joy to be with and another an absolute nightmare? How people respect themselves, get along with others, perform at school, perform at work, and connect in marriage all stems from the power of their self-image.

A healthy Self-image is not meant to be selfish or arrogant.

If you raise a strong kid who grows up with self-esteem, it ensures that they have a realistic view of their abilities and weaknesses, enjoy achievements, and focus on problem areas. If there is such a clear parallel to how the child thinks about himself and how he behaves, it is important to discipline the child positively. Your child will be subjected to positive experiences (builders) and negative factors during childhood (breakers). Parents should introduce their children to more builders and help them work through breakers.

Practice parental attachment

Put yourself in the shoes of a child who spends several hours a day in the arms of a caregiver, is held in a sling, breastfed, and her cries are immediately answered. How do you think this kid feels?

This child feels loved; this child feels precious. Have you ever had a memorable day where you got showered with praise? You probably felt very appreciative and cherished. The baby at the receiving end of this high-touch parenting approach gains self-worth. She likes what she's feeling.

Self-confidence and Self Worth

Responsiveness is the secret to building child self-esteem. E.g., the baby gives a sign of wanting to be fed or comforted. The caregiver reacts quickly. When this cue-response sequence is repeated several hundred, maybe thousands of times in the first year, the child discovers that her signals have meaning: "Someone listens to me. Therefore, I'm loved."

Of course, you can't always answer quickly. This is the primary trend that matters. You're going to have days where you're out on patience. As the child grows older, it becomes necessary for him to learn how to cope with healthy anger, which will help him adapt to change. The main thing is that you're there for him; that's the message on which the child constructs his sense of self.

Infants developing brains

We stress the importance of early Parenting because, in the first two years, the baby's brain is developing very rapidly. This is the period that a child creates patterns of connections – internal representations of how things function. The subconscious of the growing child is like a file cabinet. There is a mental image in each file of the cue she gives, along with the answer she expects. During every encounter, the child stores a cognitive memory of what happened. For example, the child lifts her arms, and the parent responds by picking her up. Repetition deepens these habits in the child's consciousness, and ultimately, feelings, good or negative, become aligned with them. A file drawer full of mainly optimistic emotions and mental images contributes to a sense of "rightness." Her sense of "well-being" becomes part of the child's self.

Attachment to Parents introduces the feeling of "well-being."

Children who get used to the sense of well-being obtained from attachment parenting spend most of their lives trying to keep the feeling alive. Since they have "feeling healthy" engraved in their subconscious, they will recover quickly from setbacks. They can fall a lot, but they're sure to rise up stronger each time. This definition is particularly true for a child who is handicapped or appears to be entering the comparatively short-lived realm of natural talent.

Children who don't have this early feeling of well-being struggle to find it, so they don't realize what they're searching for. This is why certain children who have an attachment to parents in the early years cope well despite a troubled upbringing due to family issues.

Babies are resilient, and, of course, it's never too late to start a habit that helps raise a confident child. Getting to know your kid and seeing things from their perspective will help them learn to trust themselves. This kind of Parenting cements the blocks of self-worth together. The faster the cement is added, the smoother it continues and the longer it sticks.

Improve your self-confidence

Parenting is a therapeutic activity. You also cure yourself in caring for your kids. In my work, a mother with a high-needed child once said, "My child brings out the best and the worst in me." If there are issues with your experience that concern your current parenting, confront them. Get psychiatric support if they interfere with your ability to stay calm.

Raise a Confident Kid by developing Your Self-confidence

The child's self-esteem is gained, not inherited. Certain parenting characteristics and character traits, such as anger and anxiety, are acquired in each generation. Having a child gives you the opportunity to become the mom you wish you had. If you have low self-confidence, particularly if you feel like it is the product of your parenting, take action to repair yourself and break the family cycle. Try this exercise to help raise a confident infant (therapists call it "passing on the best and discarding the rest").

- List particular things your parents did to create your self-image.
- List particular things your parents did to undermine your self-image.

Now, try to imitate the positive things your parents have done and ignore the rest. If you find it tough to follow this exercise on your own, get the assistance of a therapist. You and your child will both benefit from it.

Don't be too tough on your parents.

They did the best they could because of their conditions and the popular advice of the time. I recall hearing a grandma say to a woman once, "I was a good mother to you. I was following exactly the routine that the doctor sent me." This new mother believed that some of her present issues resulted from the strict schedule she went through while she was a child. She was determined to learn how to interpret the cues of her infant. I reminded her not to criticize her mother because the prevailing parental trend was to obey the "experts" and follow their guidance on child-rearing. However, the new mother is more relaxed as an authority figure to her offspring.

Children copy your emotional state

No one can put on a positive face all the time, but a parent's unhappiness can be passed to an infant. Your kid looks like a mirror to you regardless of his own emotions. You can't reflect positive feelings if you're not exuding positive feelings. So if you have severe issues with depression or anxiety, get treatment to overcome these symptoms before they impact your kids.

Chapter 32:
Overwhelmed Thinking

When you are experiencing mental overload, it can feel overwhelming. Many individuals have this feeling at different stages in their lives. It means being swamped by an overwhelming and unruly emotion that everything is too difficult to control. When faced with intense emotions, it can be difficult to think and behave rationally, let alone function normally. Needless to say, this sensation is painful, and the causes and consequences will affect both your personal and professional life.

What Are the Sources of Mental Overwhelm?

When a person feels the stressors are too much to handle, they become exhausted, which can be caused by various factors.

Define Being Overwhelmed

Being emotionally drained, by definition, means being submerged by your thoughts and fears for all of life's current challenges, to the point that you lack clarity and feel trapped or paralyzed. Compare the sensation of being overwhelmed to being swept away by a rogue wave. It's a terrifying experience; you do not know which way is up or which way to dive. You may be unable to think or behave rationally, and your relationships or professional life may suffer as a result. Emotional overwhelm may arise for a brief period or a far longer, depending on whether it is caused by an unusually difficult period at work, a painful personal occurrence such as losing a loved one, or some inciting factor.

The following are examples of common interactions that can contribute to emotional overwhelm:

- Relationship difficulties
- Illness, either physical or emotional
- A difficult work
- Nutritional deficiencies
- Insecurity and financial hardship
- Life-altering events
- Grief with a loved one
- Abuse and other personal traumas
- Sleep deprivation as a habit

Symptoms of Overwhelm

An oppressive feeling can show itself in several ways when a person is experiencing it. In any case, a person is more likely to be overcome by negative emotions — such as frustration, terror, anxiety, or shame — and it is often difficult to understand and verbalize the exact cause of the stress. The release of cortisol, commonly known as the "stress hormone," is the reason why a person's body overreacts. When you feel stressed, cortisol rushes into your body, leaving you with a high level of anxiety. Simultaneously, our serotonin reserves, the chemical that helps our bodies overcome stress and anxiety, continue to deplete. This mixture creates the deep sense of utter desperation that is synonymous with being overwhelmed. Overwhelm is frequently as unpleasant as it is uncontrollable. It manifests as fear, frustration, or severe irritability and concern. Doubt and helplessness can also sneak into a person's usual thought pattern. It can manifest physically when a person lashes out emotionally, cries, or has a panic attack. These sensations are often accompanied by a rapid pulse, perspiration, shortness of breath, or even chest pain.

Why am I crying too much?

When overwhelmed, some people weep. It's okay to scream! Everyone does so, but some more often than others. According to one report, women weep 30-64 times a year, while men cry 5-17 times per year. However, this gender disparity illustrates how men's weeping has become wrongly stigmatized as a form of weakness. As a result, these reports are most likely inaccurate. Crying is a good way to express our inner feelings, and it can also make us understand ourselves better. It has many benefits and can reduce discomfort, sometimes leaving one with a cathartic feeling. If you feel you weep too much, that you are inconsolable, or that your weeping interferes with your everyday life, you should see your psychiatrist. If this is the case, weeping may be a symptom of an ongoing mood illness, such as depression, or another mental health condition, such as anxiety.

Stopping or Avoiding Cognitive Overwhelm

Whatever the source, if you have symptoms of overwhelm, there are certain things you can do on your own and with the help of others.

1. Acknowledge the depressive thoughts.

Fighting off all-consuming feelings is unlikely to help you relax in a stressful situation. Know that fear is a "natural" aspect of human life and use acceptance as a way to move through those unpleasant feelings (when possible).

2. Reverse the stressed-out thought patterns

Feelings of unpredictability and utter depression fuel overwhelm. These nonsensical feelings accumulate as fear and may cause considerable pain. Stop the pessimistic feelings before they become habitual ruminations. Simultaneously, continue to think of alternatively more optimistic ideas.

3. Take some deep breaths.

When you actively breathe in deeply, you trigger your body's calming reflex, which can be useful in intense situations. Additionally, as each movement lets you concentrate your breath, performing yoga, meditation, and gradual muscle-relaxing will help ease your body's reaction to anxiety.

4. Be present in the moment

Consider one moment, job, or event at a time, in the present moment, to help minimize the risk of uncontrollable feelings that may or may not occur.

5. Do more research

Aside from breathing and meditation exercises for preventing overwhelm, there is a wealth of scientific literature about how stress and anxiety affect our cognitive ability. Discover what research and advice resonate with you by using online search resources to improve your ability to handle certain emotions.

Chapter 33:
Body Shaming

What exactly is body shaming? "We are our own biggest critic" is a term we often use to explain when we are excessively critical of ourselves. Most people have a normal drive to be better, quicker, and healthier. Still, this fascination with being better may have significant mental health effects, particularly when it comes to our physical appearances. The media has also depicted overweight characters as the show's running gag, resulting in "fat jokes" and a serious form of self-doubt known as body shaming. Body shaming is described as the activity or practice of publicly humiliating another person's body shape or size; it is a type of bullying that can cause extreme emotional distress, particularly in children. Body shaming is practiced by parents, siblings, colleagues, rivals, and classmates. "What is she wearing? It is not attractive in the least." Self-bashing ideas and sentences like, "I am so ugly in comparison to her that I will never have a date," and "I am so ugly in comparison to her that I will never find a husband." Negative comments about someone's body image or shape may be highly detrimental to their mental health, ultimately leading to low self-esteem, rage, self-harm, and in worse cases, suicide.

Both men and women of all ages and sizes experience body shaming. Body shaming has featured criticisms of being "too fat" or "too thin," often dwelling on entirely insignificant shortcomings. Often, magazines, social media sites, and commercials lead to body shaming in ways that normalize these harmful habits. Many TV shows and movies have followed suit, with the "fat" character usually serving as ridicule and comedic relief. With celebrity weight shaming on social media becoming more common, it is crucial to consider the possible implications.

How to Get Rid of Body Shaming

Like every other kind of bullying, body shaming will still exist until you stand up for yourself constructively and safely. It is important to practice self-love to resist allowing derogatory remarks to annoy you. If you see body shaming on social media, you should report it and mark it as offensive content. The National Eating Disorder Association (NEDA) has stepped up its efforts to combat body shaming on social media and urges individuals who experience body shaming to report it to this organization through the Media Watchdog network. You may also start a petition against body shaming, write a body-positive post or blog, and so on.

Chapter 34:
Myths about raising an anxious child

The most challenging part of parenting a child with an anxiety disorder is the persistent occurrence of anxiety-related misconceptions. Whether personally or professionally, everyone you meet appears to have an opinion, but seldom does anybody know the truth. Myths about anxiety abound, and all of them are harshly dismissive of those who suffer from it. If you identify with these anxiety misconceptions as a parent or have no idea what anxiety problems are, learning the truth opens your heart and mind to those who suffer from this condition.

Anxiety is very rare in children and teens.

Unfortunately, anxiety disorders in children are widespread, and the number of children diagnosed is increasing. According to CDC (the Centers for Disease Control and Prevention), anxiety disorder affects 7.1% of children aged 3-17 years (approximately 4.4 million).

That means that 7-8 out of every 100 children have anxiety disorder. This excludes children who have anxiety but have not been diagnosed with an illness.

Children's fear is the product of a deficient upbringing.

Anxiety is a hereditary predisposition that a person inherits. Not all children who are predisposed to fear will experience anxiety, but those who do may do so due to various reasons.

Parents need to understand their part in parenting an anxious child, but you can never believe that you are the source of your child's anxiety.

A child will stop being nervous if he or she desires.

Anxiety is not a logical feeling that can be suppressed. No child or teenager needs and wants to feel afraid. When someone advises a kid to "stop getting nervous," "calm down," or "just relax," he or she is assuming that this is an emotion that can be turned off. That is just not how it works.

No amount of clarification from a parent or caregiver would be enough to persuade a child to toggle off the anxiety.

An anxious child is weak and lazy.

Quite the contrary. Children and teenagers who suffer from anxiety are courageous and hardworking. They wake up every day with their heads full of unpleasant thoughts and emotions. It takes real bravery to go through life feeling burdened by frightening, unsettling feelings.

And when fear takes hold, and an infant or adolescent withdraws shies away from people, vulnerability and laziness are not to blame. They cannot get past their fear, both mentally and physically, since they lack the necessary skills and resources.

Shy anxious children and teens

A child or adolescent suffering from anxiety, such as social anxiety, is filled with self-doubt and confusion, leaving them unable to communicate with others in some circumstances. These children desire to communicate and converse with people, but their fear prevents them from doing so. This is not shyness; rather, it is fear.

Many children and teenagers want to engage with their classmates, comfortably walk down the school hallways, attend gatherings or sports, and do various other things, but their fear prevents them from doing so.

Anxiety appears the same.

Anxiety is as distinct as the infant or teenager experiencing it. Anxiety can present itself in children and adolescents as clinginess, crying, or hiding. It can manifest itself in others as anger, avoidance, or defiance. Some people suffer physical symptoms such as trembling, stomachache, heavy breathing, or an elevated heart rate, while others do not.

It is important to mention that, while they can suffer from anxiety, your child or teenager can communicate their anxiety in many different ways.

Even within the same child or teenager, the response to anxiety can change based on the situation that is causing the stress.

Anxiety is not real; it is a child's dramatic behavior.

Anxiety is very real, whether or not a known anxiety condition has been diagnosed. Anxiety-related thinking and emotions may be almost paralyzing, resulting in habitual negative loops. An infant or adolescent can do about anything to escape anxiety-inducing conditions, which sometimes manifests as misbehavior.

Anxiety may become dramatic as an infant or adolescent attempts to regain composure after an unpleasant encounter. When faced with an anxiety-inducing situation, they can boss people around, protest, moan, or whine. These are all attempts by the infant to stop or overcome the fear.

When an infant or adolescent complains of medical problems, they are actually experiencing them. It is not just in their minds.

The importance of debunking anxiety myths

Being aware of the realities around anxiety, instead of commonly accepted misconceptions, helps you better understand and support an insecure child or teenager when they need it the most. Many well-intended remarks and suggestions may be detrimental to an unhappy child or adolescent. There is no easy way to give comfort to an infant or adolescent at their most vulnerable, but by understanding the truth of fear, you are one step closer to being able to help.

NOTES

Printed in Great Britain
by Amazon